THE SITCOM WRITER'S COOKBOOK

Your Recipe for TV Writing Success

KEVIN KELTON

Kelton Media LLC

THE SITCOM WRITER'S COOKBOOK

© 2022 Kelton Media LLC
ISBN-13: 979-8804649426
ASIN: B09Y4LDJ95

Cover Chef Image: Depositphotos #306054184 Dated 12-24-2023

FAIR USE NOTICE

WHAT WRITERS ARE SAYING ABOUT THIS BOOK

"The best book on sitcom writing from one of the best writers I know. Kevin gives you everything you need to create an entertaining, memorable sitcom. I wish this book was around when I was starting out. It's a winner."
—Bruce Kirschbaum, *Seinfeld, Everybody Loves Raymond*

"You can't teach funny, but Kevin Kelton can teach everything else about the sitcom universe. Read this book and then get cookin' on your killer pilot or spec script."
–Doug McIntyre, *Married With Children, WKRP in Cincinnati*

"Kevin is brilliant in that area. He's a must read if you plan on writing sitcoms."
—Tom Dreesen, standup comedian

"This is a fabulous book for sitcom writers. Concise, to the point, funny and very understandable."
—Amazon Reader Review

AUTHOR'S TV CREDITS

SATURDAY NIGHT LIVE
BOY MEETS WORLD
NIGHT COURT
A DIFFERENT WORLD
SOMETHING SO RIGHT
SHAKY GROUND
THE TOM SHOW (STARRING TOM ARNOLD)
THE VAN DYKE SHOW
KNIGHT AND DAYE
WOMEN IN PRISON
THE JAY LENO SPECIAL
TWILIGHT THEATER
THE JEFFERSONS
LAUGH TRAX
FRIDAYS
Plus, pilots for F/X and HBO

AUTHOR'S NOTE

Welcome to this how-to guide to television half-hour comedy writing.

Throughout this book I reference links to various television episodes and other instructive material for your convenience. Some of those are printed in the Resources section at the back of the book, others are links you can use to find the material online. Those links all worked when I wrote the book. However, I have noticed that, over time, a link can often go dead or be removed for intellectual property rights reasons. If some of the links in this book don't work for you, that's why. Such is life when you are using the internet for resources. But you can still do a web search for the material and, with a bit of ingenuity and perseverance, you can often find it on your own.

Some of the scripts, outlines and beat sheets referenced thought out the book may also be found at https://kevinkelton. com/links. Bu

But, we all know that links that worked yesterday may not work tomorrow. **So, if you cannot access one of the**

Assignment items at that link, substitute it with another beat sheet, outline or TV script you can find online. Drew's Script-O-Rama, The Script Lab, DailyScript.com and other sites like them can provide a ton of excellent reading material.

In the pages to come, I'll cover the do's and don'ts of writing spec scripts for existing TV series, composing an original pilot of your own, and writing the comedy screenplay. The methodology is fairly similar. Pilot scripts offer a lot more creative freedom than series specs, but also a lot more headaches, as you don't have a pre-existing "world" of characters and environments (home, workplace, etc.) from which to borrow.

Movies offer the most creative freedom of all. And the most Hollywood prestige...*if* you can get one made.

And while we'll have some fun with the cookbook parallels, I'm dead serious about helping you turn out the best script(s) you have in you. Just trust the process and do the work. I'll squeeze your creative juices and simmer the God-given talents you have until you're whipping up professional quality scripts on your own.

Don't worry. I won't take the "cookbook" metaphor too far.

One final thought before we jump in. You'll notice that many of the examples I use in this book are classic network sitcoms from days past, and you may wonder if their lessons still apply in the age of Netflix and Hulu. The answer is a definitive "yes!" While humor and storytelling styles have evolved, basic story structure and character dynamics have not. You can learn as much from an episode of *The Mary Tyler Moore Show* as you can from *PEN15* or *Call My Agent*. (Or whatever happens to be hot when you're reading this.)

Robert McKee, the leading screenwriting guru of our time, uses *Casablanca* (1942) as his primary film example, and refers to *Chinatown* (1974) and *Butch Cassidy & the Sundance Kid* (1969) liberally in his best-selling screenwriting books and seminars. Similarly, Aaron Sorkin's popular "Master Class" relies on *A Few Good Men* (1992) and *All The President's Men* (1976).

Which is why I strongly recommend you watch or read classic pilots like *Friends, Roseanne, Home Improvement, Cosby, Taxi, The Mary Tyler Moore Show,* and *Everybody Loves Raymond* to see how great TV scripts are written. Great is great, be it on CBS in the 1980s, or Netflix in the 2020s.

INTRODUCTION

Meet the Head Chef

On the set of NIGHT COURT with Harry Anderson

By now, you've already seen a few of my credits on the cover and you've probably Googled me or gone to IMDB to see the full list. But here's a little more detail about my writing background and why you should listen to anything I say.

I started out as a stand-up comedian and joke writer for Joan Rivers and lots of lesser-known comics. Actually, I got my start writing material for my brother, Bobby Kelton, who began doing stand-up in the LA and NY comedy clubs in the mid-70s. While hanging out with him, I also got to meet and hangout with people like Larry David, Jerry Seinfeld, Jay Leno, and dozens of other stand-ups who never got quite that famous but were still amazingly funny. By hanging out with them backstage and at coffee shops after their shows, I learned how to bounce premises, hone wording, and formulate comedy bits and routines. I was going to comedy college and didn't even know it.

After graduating from real college (with a degree in Business Administration), I drove across country and began doing stand-up and selling lines to anyone who'd buy from me. Joan Rivers and Tom Dreesen bought lines from me. A pre-fame David Letterman wanted to buy a line of mine, but we couldn't agree on a price. In retrospect, I should've just sold it to him. The credit would've been worth a lot more. But, while I was saving the best material for my own act, I soon realized that writing was my gift and what I loved to do. So, that's the career I pursued.

My first TV writing job was on a game show. Soon after I stepped up to writing for a string of sketch comedy shows, including two seasons on *Saturday Night Live*.

After a few more years in sketch writing, including specials for Steve Martin and Jay Leno, I finally – after eleven spec scripts – broke into sitcoms. I began as a staff writer on a very unmemorable Dick Van Dyke series and moving up the ladder until I was the co-executive producer of a very

Kevin performing on SNL with Gary Kroger (R)

unmemorable Tom Arnold series. (Both great guys, though.) Some of the better-known half-hour shows I worked on were *Boy Meets World* for ABC; *Night Court, A Different World,* and *Something So Right* for NBC; *The Jeffersons* and the afore-mentioned Dick Van Dyke series for CBS; and *Shaky Ground* and *Women in Prison* for FOX. In the days before streaming services, I wrote for all five major networks: ABC, NBC, CBS, FOX, and The WB plus F/X and HBO. There was an Emmy nomination and a Humanitas Prize in there someplace. Not a bad run!

Along the way, I worked with tons of talented people (measured in tons partially due to their eating habits), learned how to structure a script, and turn amusing thoughts into audience laughter. (One doesn't always follow the other.)

With Markie Post of *NIGHT COURT*

Most importantly for you, I ran writing staffs and learned how to mentor novice writers. I've taught television and film writing at the university level and for the UCLA Extension Writers' Program. My students have won competitions, and some have gone on to work as professional writers.

So, my method is tested. It works. It has worked for others, and it can work for you.

Now, let's get to cooking up some great comedy scripts. Bon appétit!

BREAKING STORIES

Appetizers

BREAKING STORIES

1

RECIPE FOR SUCCESS

INGREDIENTS:
- DETERMINATION
- STUDYING THE HALF-HOUR ART FORM
- IDEAS
- TALENT
- MORE DETERMINATION

Hopefully you are already a fan of the half-hour TV comedy format. This book will start your journey from spectator to player. The first thing to understand is that the current market-place really doesn't differentiate between types of sitcoms.

At one time in the 1980s and 90s, it was in vogue to qualify a show as a taped sitcom, filmed sitcom, multi-camera, single-camera, dramedy, seriocomedy, and other awkwardly named sub-genres that rarely had uniform meanings or parameters. (Imagine having to tell people you were a dramedy writer.)

These days we just use the umbrella term "sitcom". A throwback to the 50s and 60s catch-all phrase "situation comedy" that was used to describe a family show (*I Love Lucy* or *The Honeymooners*), a workplace series (*F-Troop* or *Get Smart*), or a high-concept series (*Bewitched* or *Gilligan's Island*). In this book the term "sitcom" refers to any scripted half-hour comedy series.

More recently we've had sitcoms about domestic life: *Blackish, The Goldbergs, Family Guy*, workplaces: *Ted Lasso, Mr. Mayor, Brooklyn Nine-Nine* and concept-driven series: *Schitt's Creek, The Marvelous Mrs. Maisel, The Good Life, Hacks*. Few series are shot in front of a live studio audience anymore. (Though some Disney and Nick shows still shoot live.) This has greatly changed the style and pacing of sitcoms, as shows are no longer limited in the number of sets or scenes they can use in one episode. Taped shows typically had only 4-5 sets and each scene was 3-4 minutes or longer. Today's half-hour shows can have a dozen or more scenes and sets, with some as short as 20 seconds.

Networks, Outlets and Platforms

Another thing that has changed is the length of a sitcom episode. In the structure of **network** and **basic cable** sitcoms, an episode is generally 22 minutes long (not counting commercials) and is broken up into two or three acts, sometimes with a cold opening and/or a tag at the end. On **paid cable networks** and **streaming services**, a half-hour episode is 28 minutes or longer and has no commercial breaks. Therefore no "act breaks" in the script. And then there are web-based series that defy all the rules.

But whether you chose to outline a network show like *The Simpsons* or a paid cable show like *Barry* that doesn't have commercial breaks, we'll still use the basic two or three act narrative structure. The casual TV viewer may not discern the distinction, but professional readers – the producers, TV executives, and agents who will be judging your writing – will definitely know if this structure is there or not.

Regardless of whether you're writing a network series or pay cable series, the general structure of a sitcom *story* has not changed much in 50 years.

Half-hour comedy scripts are generally broken into an "A-story" and a "B-story." The A-story is the main plot, and it runs the course of the episode. The B-story is a subplot and is usually subservient to the A-story. Some series use A, B and C-plot structures, where the C-story is just a runner, or a few related bits used to service characters and get a little extra comedy into the episode. C-stories don't need to be as complete as A and B-stories; often they are just runners with no ending. The *30 Rock* script we'll be looking at in the first couple of chapters, titled "SeinfeldVision," has two C-runners. If all this A/B/C talk is gobble-de-gook now, don't worry, it will become clear as we get into it.

So how do we develop A and B-stories and pair them together? This, frankly, is the art of sitcom writing (along with great dialog). An A-story is any plot that you believe you can string into a solid 12–18-minute story, with a unique hook, a clear inciting incident, a compelling act break, and a climax that the audience won't see coming. (We'll talk in more detail about each of these story elements later in the book.) Your B-story should utilize regular series characters who aren't in your A-plot and have enough meat to fill 6-8 minutes of the episode (at least 3-5 scenes).

What is a hook, you ask? Good question. The hook is something that will make your episode stand out and be unique. In *Family Guy* it could be something as bold as Stewie and Brian going to a parallel universe or the entire episode being a *Star Wars* parody. In *The Office* it might be a baby shower at Dwight's farm with a Renaissance Faire theme. Or the hook may simply be an A-story that focuses on a minor character like Toby or Creed.

When I develop stories for spec scripts, I try to come up with a memorable hook, since I want the reader to remember my script over the hundreds of others they have read every season. For one spec, I matched two NBC series together and wrote a combination *Just Shoot Me* and *News Radio*, using both series' characters and sets. In my *Mad About You* spec, I had Paul and Jamie leave NY City for a week of housesitting in suburbia. Both scripts got great reactions, landed me staff jobs and were remembered by people who read them years later.

Your story doesn't need a heavy hook. But you should always try to make your spec script unique and memorable so it stands out in the marketplace. Remember, the series' producers don't need people who can write *as well as* their current staff – they already have those. They want new blood who can write their show *better than their current staff!*

Homework (if you call this 'work')

This week, I want you to watch one (or hopefully more) sitcom episodes and look for the A and B-stories. You may not be able to discern them at first, or you may find a show with no apparent B-story or with multiple C-subplots.

After you watch an episode, write down what show you watched and what the A-story and B-story were. Tell each story in **no more than** a sentence or two.

Example: (From the *30 Rock* episode, "SeinfeldVision"):

A-STORY: JACK IS TRYING TO BEEF UP NBC'S RATINGS BY DIGI-TALLY INSERTING JERRY SEINFELD INTO EVERY SERIES. BUT

WHEN AN ANGRY SEINFELD SHOWS UP AT 30 ROCK TO STOP HIM, JACK MUST AVOID JERRY UNTIL HE CAN FIND A SOLUTION.

B-STORY: CERIE ASKS LIZ AND JENNA TO BE HER BRIDES-MAIDS, SENDING LIZ INTO A SINGLE-WITH-NO-PROSPECTS PANIC ATTACK.

This episode also has two C-runners (a Tracy-Kenneth office marriage story and a Jenna overeating story). But for now, all you need to identify in the show you watch are the A and B-stories.

In the next chapter, you'll choose a series to write. Then you'll come up with a few potential A and B-stories for your show. But for now, just focus on being able to identify the A-B-C stories in an existing episode and put them into a short TV Guide style description.

ASSIGNMENT
WATCH AND READ – THE *30 ROCK* EPISODE, "SEINFELD VISION" (WRITTEN BY TINA FEY).

VIDEO: HTTPS://CUTT.LY/SEINFELDVISION
SCRIPT: HTTPS://WWW.KEVINKELTON.COM/LINKS

NOTE THAT BECAUSE IT'S A PRODUCTION SCRIPT, IT WILL HAVE FORMATTING ELEMENTS THAT SPEC SCRIPTS SHOULD NOT HAVE, LIKE CAST AND LOCATIONS LISTS, AND SHOT NUMBERS. EVEN IF YOU VIEW THE EPISODE FIRST, I STILL RECOMMEND THAT YOU READ THE SCRIPT. TO LEARN THIS CRAFT, VIEWING SHOWS IS NO SUBSTITUTE FOR READING SCRIPTS.

WATCH – ONE HALF-HOUR COMEDY EPISODE OF YOUR CHOICE. WHAT WAS THE A-STORY OF THE EPISODE YOU WATCHED? WHAT WAS THE B-STORY?

STARTERS: THEMES AND IDEAS

INGREDIENTS:

-1 CURRENT TV SERIES YOU'D LIKE TO WRITE

-1 THEME YOU'D LIKE TO EXPLORE IN YOUR SCRIPT

-1 TO 2 STORY IDEAS THAT SUPPORT THAT THEME

-6 OR MORE WATCHED EPISODES OF YOUR SERIES

-2 TO 3 PRODUCED SCRIPTS (READ PRIOR TO WRITING)

-1 CREATIVE MIND (OR TWO IF YOU ARE A TEAM)

Themes

Before you can tell a good story, you have to know what your story is about. That is your theme. Some novice writers confuse a theme with a premise. They think, "My story is about a guy who works at a used car lot but is secretly a foreign spy." No, that's a premise.

What his story is about might be, "Even the lowliest guy in the neighborhood can change the world" or "The fortunes of mankind can rise and fall on one man's character." *That's a theme.*

And every good TV and film story should have one, even an episode of *Family Guy*.

So, decide what you want to say about the world through the story you want to tell. Then write that idea in a single, declarative sentence or a question. For instance, *"In a world of Tinder and hookups, can a devoted virgin still find love?"* is a theme posed as a question.

Look in the book's Resources section in the back for a list of TV pilot themes. While these apply to an entire series, you should try to come up with a declarative theme for your spec episode. It will give your plot subtext and impact, and make your script stand out from the spec crowd.

A-stories

In the previous chapter, we talked about the A/B story structure. This time, we're going to dive a little deeper into A-stories and B-stories and what makes them tick.

First off, remember that the story you're writing is about 22 minutes long (28 if you're writing for a cable series or streaming service with no commercial breaks) and 30-35 pages in screenplay format. As a rule of thumb, your A-story will comprise a little over half of that. So, you have to have a story that holds up for at least 12 to 14 minutes and 17 pages.

When I first come up with a story idea, I usually don't know how "full" it is or if it's a legitimate A-story or not. But I trust the process and know that if I keep working the idea, it will expand and take life. You will learn to trust your instincts, too, as you write more spec scripts and get the feel for what makes an A-story and what doesn't. (Remember, I wrote eleven of those suckers before I landed my first half-hour staff writing job.)

We start with the basics: beginning, middle and end. How will the story start? Does it have any twists or interesting escalations? Do you know where it's going, and is it worth going there?

If I have a movie idea about a psychiatrist treating a boy who sees ghosts and, in the end, he convinces the boy that there are no ghosts, the story doesn't sound all that compelling. But if in the end the psychiatrist learns that *he's* a ghost who's been dead all along, well, I write it and I'm rich! (Hope that didn't spoil anything for anyone.)

Not every story is going to have a big surprise ending, but they all have to have a *satisfying* ending. The down-and-out boxer can lose the title bout as long as he gains something, and the audience enjoys the journey. You're taking the audience on a trip, and you better make it one they want to go on.

Okay, so you've got a starting point and a destination. Now you need to plan a few interesting stops along the way. Have you ever noticed that the best vacation trips are the ones that don't go exactly as you planned it? (Are you getting tired of the travel metaphors yet?)

A good story is a planned trip gone bad. The character driving the story – let's use Jack in *30 Rock's* "SeinfeldVision" – thinks he's got a brilliant idea (digitally inserting Jerry Seinfeld into every NBC show) and at the end of his trip, he's going to see ratings skyrocket and his network thrive. What he didn't plan on is Jerry returning from Europe and learning what Jack is up to. Jack's trip has taken an unexpected turn for the worse. That's an act break.

Some half-hour series are written in two acts, some in three, and occasionally four (with a long cold opening being the de facto first act). Check the structure of the series you are writing to know which they use. But even if you are writing a cable series like *Dexter* or a streaming series like *After Life, Hacks* or *Master of None*, it's best to build in an act break or two. It will make your structure stronger. Even if those act breaks are imperceptible to the average viewer. You don't have to label them as Act One and Act Two in your script if your series doesn't use that script format. But you should know where the natural act breaks fall for your own clarity and efficacy.

On many streaming series, you can actually see the built-in commercial breaks when a scene fades to black for two seconds. That is where they intend the commercials to play if the series is ever sold into syndication.

For a more in-depth look at the difference between act breaks and commercial breaks, see Chapter 25.

Elements of an A-story

Let's assume you've got a story idea that you think is intriguing, has a good twist or two along the way, and a pretty good ending. That sounds like an A-story. But there's a couple of more things you need to ask yourself:

- Does it use the series characters in a fun or new way?
- Does the character grow in some way? Does it advance his/her series arc? Will he/she be a better (or worse) person at the end of the episode than they were at the end of last week's show? (If it's Jack Donaghy, Deborah Vance, or Archie Bunker, they can be worse and it's still a satisfying conclusion.)
- Is this a story the series hasn't told yet, but should have?
- Will the actors like what they're doing in this story? (Very important if you are already on staff of the show.)
- Will the network think this episode is promotable? (Notice I didn't say "this story is promotable." The network doesn't care about the story, they care about the episode. NBC might think a story about Jack stealing someone's intellectual property is too highbrow. But add a guest spot by Jerry Seinfeld, and all of a sudden, it's ratings gold.)

Those are all subjective questions, and your "yes" answers may be another person's "no."

But if **you** believe in it, go with it. After all, what you're selling (aside from your writing skills and comedy chops) is your creative point-of-view. If it's unique, you'll succeed. So bet on yourself.

Side note: Over my years as a TV writer and producer, I read lots of scripts I thought stunk. I thought they were unfunny, unprofessional, and sometimes a frightening glimpse into the writer's mental instability. Most of the time I was right. But a few times I was extremely wrong, and that writer went on to great success. I also had so-called experts tell *ME* I was wasting my time trying to write for TV when I was first starting out. And *they* were extremely wrong! So, if you believe in your talent, go with it. Look, if you're not talented, you're going to fail either way. But if you truly have a talent that's unique, you have to go with your instincts. Every successful writer will tell you so.

Inciting Incidents

Every story starts some place. A good story has a clear and powerful inciting incident.

To understand this concept, imagine a long row of dominos. Now imagine a hand knocking the first domino down, which will lead to all the others falling in line. That first domino is the inciting incident.

The best example is *Rocky*. Apollo Creed's next opponent just broke his thumb and Apollo needs a new chump to beat up on. Rocky isn't even in the room when the inciting incident happens. But we know the story (and Rocky's life) just took a huge turn.

Once you figure out the beginning and end of your story, and maybe a few of the plot turns along the way, figure out what your inciting incident is. That is the moment when the character's day (and maybe life) is going to change for better or worse. They may not know it, but we the viewers should know it.

It can be small (the babysitter just cancelled) or it can be huge (Jerry Seinfeld shows up to spoil your plans). But every good episode has one.

If possible, try to get your inciting incident as an action that happens in the body of your script (not in backstory or exposition). The earlier, the better. Of course, there are exceptions to every rule. *Rocky* being a great example - that inciting incident didn't happen until 25 minutes into the movie (pages 30-34 in the screenplay). But as a rule of thumb, keep your inciting incident early and on screen. **Seeing** something happen makes the sharpest plot point.

Think of your story as a long, intricate dominos design. Seeing them go down will look great, but to be really satisfying, you want to see it start with that finger poking the first domino. Your inciting incident is the finger poke. Show it.

Block Comedy Scenes

This is a slightly archaic term, but some shows and writers still use it, so I want you to be familiar with it.

A **block comedy scene** is a scene that exists to be (pardon my French) balls-out funny. In older sitcoms the block comedy scene was a big site gag or visual comedy scene, usually in the second act. The classic example is Lucy working on the chocolate factory conveyor belt, and the chocolates start coming too fast for her to handle.

Today series don't rely on one big comedy scene – the whole script should be darn funny – but as I said, some writers and network executives still use the term and look for the block comedy scene in a script.

So, make sure you have something big and really funny someplace in your second act – something visual or very weird/absurd.

Then if anyone asks *where's your block comedy scene?* Point to that, and you'll be covered.

B-stories

Okay, back to our topic: stories. We've discussed the elements of a good A-story. What about a good B-story?

Well, if it has all the elements of a good A-story, it might also make a good B-story, but why waste it? Usually a series' B-stories come from those ideas that are really funny and unique but can't support an entire episode because they're missing one or more key element. My B-stories generally come from a funny idea that has no compelling twists or big resolution. It's just an idea for a few scenes that I think would balance out the A-plot. If I have an A-story that's more on the serious side, I look for a B that is very broad. If I have an A-story that I really like but it doesn't service one or more key characters, I look to balance it with a B-plot that services those actors. (Nothing kills a table read[1] like a star who has less lines or gets less laughs than the supporting actors.)

Someplace in the A or B-story, there also should be a hook: something that's so unique and promotable that the producers (and network) will definitely want to tell that story. Maybe it's a side of one character that we've never seen before. Maybe it's something in the news or the current zeitgeist. Maybe it's a way of telling a conventional story in an unconventional way (as Quentin Tarantino did in *Pulp Fiction* and *Reservoir Dogs*). Send Peter Griffin into Amish country and you've got a hook. It creates a curiosity and expectation in the viewers that will (hopefully) compel them to tune in.

To paraphrase the famous Potter Stewart line about pornography, I can't define what a good hook is, but I know it when I see it.

C-Stories (Runners)

While sitcoms of 20 years ago used to suffice with just an A and B-story, today's shows use more sophisticated storytelling.

That can mean two B-stories, or an A-story, B-story and multiple C-stories (also called "runners"). Some shows use highly sophisticated structures, which we'll be covering in more depth in a later chapter.

C-stories (or "runners") are generally just a small running gag throughout the episode. They may be totally separate from the A and B-stories, or they may be integrated into them. Pretty often a C-story doesn't have an arc or an ending, it's just a gag or character trait that is called back a couple of times. And quite often they are only there because one or two of the regular characters were left out of the main stories and the producers wanted to give them something to do.

But don't focus on your C-story yet. For now, just know the structure of the series you're writing, whether A/B/C or something even more dense. You don't have to show your C-stories in your log line, but you can start thinking about one or two that will compliment your main story lines (servicing characters that are light in the other stories and bringing hard laughs to the episode).

Loglines

A logline is sort of the TV Guide encapsulation of what the episode is about.

A good story should be able to be turned into a good logline. Here's the TVGuide.com logline for "SeinfeldVision":

As the 30 Rockers return from summer hiatus, Liz continues her battles with Jack, whose latest ploy involves inserting clips from "Seinfeld" into current shows, an act that doesn't sit well with one Jerry

SEINFELD (WHO APPEARS AS HIMSELF). MEANWHILE, JENNA
SEES HER WAISTLINE WIDEN AFTER STARRING IN THE PLAY
"MYSTIC PIZZA: THE MUSICAL!"

In the old days, when TV Guide was an actual magazine that
people bought and read, loglines were shorter and to the point,
and they rarely included the B-story. The old-time logline for
"SeinfeldVision" might have been:

WHEN JACK INSERTS OLD CLIPS OF JERRY SEINFELD INTO NBC
SHOWS, JERRY SHOWS UP TO SET HIM STRAIGHT.

Short and catchy. However, TV Guide was also in the business
of promoting viewership, so they often wrote loglines that
focused on the hook but not on the story.

The story is not about Jerry showing up – that's the hook. The
story is what Jack does once Jerry shows up. (He hides, he lies, he
brainstorms, he begs Liz for help, and he negotiates a deal.)

Key point: don't mistake your hook for your story. A good
hook may get viewers to tune in this week. A good story gets
them to come back *next week*.

Pitching

If you are fortunate enough to get a chance to get a freelance
pitch meeting for a TV series, or to be on staff and pitch to your
bosses, you'll want to create a logline for each story.

But it has to be better than a TV Guide logline. It has to tell
the beginning and end of the story, and why it will be funny. All in
2-3 sentences! For "SeinfeldVision" it might have been:

WHAT IF JACK STARTS USING JERRY SEINFELD'S IMAGE IN NEW
NBC SHOWS, AND JERRY COMES BACK FROM HIS SUPER-SECRET
VACATION MECCA IN EUROPE TO STOP HIM. JACK PANICS, HIDES

WHEN JERRY SHOWS UP, MAKES LIZ GIVE JERRY A STUDIO TOUR TO DELAY HIM, AND FINALLY HAS TO NEGOTIATE A DEAL WITH SEINFELD TO GET HIS PERMISSION AND ALSO THE NAME OF THE SECRET VACATION DESTINATION THAT ONLY JERRY AND OTHER A-LIST STARS KNOW ABOUT. (IT'S CALLED GRENYARNIA.)

Notice a couple of things:

- I started with "What if...." Not every pitch has to begin that way, but I like it because it starts the listener imagining the story in their mind.
- I added the secret vacation place to the pitch because it gives me laugh lines within the story. And it's an inside-Hollywood joke that I think the producers will chuckle at.
- I told them what happens *after the hook*. (TV Guide loglines don't do this.)
- I showed them how Liz is involved and where the humor is.
- I ended with a laugh.

Okay, so let's pretend that I was there on staff. I pitched that to the executive producers, and they liked it. (Big ifs, but go with me.) Now they say, *"That could be an A-story...the network would plotz for it! But what do we marry it to?"* (Assuming they talk like cigar-chomping 60-year-old New Yorkers from the 1960s.)

I say, *"Well, I had another idea about Cerie asking Liz and Jenna to be bridesmaids at her wedding and they have to shop for bridesmaids dresses. And that sends Liz into a single gal crisis of confidence that's so bad, she ends up buying a wedding dress in the hope of using it someday."*

Then one of the producers says, *"Hey, you know what would be funny? If Liz has to give Jerry a studio tour in the wedding dress.* Then someone else blurts out, *And, she starts crying over her effed-up love life, making her voice rise like a bad Seinfeld impression. And Jerry gets insulted!"* Everyone starts laughing, we flesh out a few more beats, making sure that all the main characters have something to do in the episode, and boom! – we have "story approval."

Does that mean the story has been approved? No, it means I'm approved to go write the outline. And the real work begins!

ASSIGNMENT

READ THE *VEEP* OUTLINE FOR THE FIRST SEASON EPISODE, "CATHERINE" (WRITTEN BY SEAN GRAY, ARMANDO IANNUCCI AND TONY ROCHE) THAT CAN BE FOUND AT HTTPS://KEVINKEL TON.COM/LINKS

WRITE – MATCH ONE OF YOUR A-STORIES TO ONE B-STORY AND WRITE A 2-3 SENTENCE LOG LINE THAT INCORPORATES BOTH PLOTS. TRY TO TELL A BEGINNING, MIDDLE AND END FOR EACH LONGLINE.

WRITE – THE THEME OF YOUR EPISODE ON A POST-IT NOTE. ONCE YOU'RE HAPPY WITH IT, STICK IT ON THE VERY EDGE OF YOUR COMPUTER SCREEN WHERE YOU CAN SEE WHILE YOU WRITE. ONCE WE GET TO THE OUTLINE AND SCRIPT STAGE OF THE PROCESS, YOU'LL WANT TO INFUSE THAT THEME INTO AS MANY SCENES AND STORY ARCS AS YOU CAN. IF YOU CAN COMPOSE A SCRIPT IN WHICH EACH STORYLINE TOUCHES ON THE SAME THEME, YOU WILL HAVE A MUCH RICHER (AND MORE SALABLE) SCRIPT.

---

1. The "table read" is the first cold reading of the script by the cast. It's done around a long table with the producers, writers, director, department leads, and network & studio executives looking on. Afterward, the writers get notes from the director and the suits (and maybe the stars), and the rewriting begins.

SMALL TASTES: THE BEAT SHEET

INGREDIENTS:

-1 EPISODE THEME

-2 TO 3 PLOTS/SUBPLOTS (DENOTED AS A/B/C STORIES)

-1 LOGLINE OR ELEVATOR PITCH

-3 MAIN CHARACTERS (ONE FOR EACH STORYLINE)

-1 INCITING INCIDENT

-1 GOAL FOR EACH MAIN CHARACTER

-1 OR MORE OBSTACLES TO EACH GOAL

-3 TO 6 ESCALATIONS OR TWISTS

-1 TO 2 SATISFYING RESOLUTIONS (ONE FOR THE A-STORY; ONE FOR THE B-STORY)

-ADD GUEST CHARACTERS AS DESIRED

The Writing Begins

You should by now know what your A and B-stories are and have the logline. It took a bit of prose writing to get it down on paper, but mostly those two steps were about thinking and being creative.

Now you begin to write stuff.

The process begins with the **beat sheet** – a list of scenes in your story, with bullet points for each "beat" of the story. A beat is the smallest unit of a story – a moment of action or dialogue that advances the story. If your story is a ladder, the beats are the rungs. The space between the rungs will be filled later with jokes, dialogue, and transitions.

Another way to think of the beat sheet is as a Powerpoint of your script – a bulleted presentation that reads easily and is quickly digested. If you were a staff writer for a series, the producers would have to sign off on the beat sheet before you begin to write the outline. (Networks generally do not review the beat sheet, though they do review and approve the outline.)

Some people like to type out their beat sheet, some prefer to handwrite it on index cards. Both work well.

The Card Method

Let's look at the card method. Get a handful of 3x5 index cards and begin to think of what will happen in your story and where. When you come up with a potential scene – say, in Jack Donaghy's NBC office – write it on the card. Then start jotting down story beats as you think of them. First, put down your inciting incident on a card, like this:

JACK'S OFFICE

- JACK TELLS LIZ ABOUT SEINFELD VISION

Then put your 1st act break on another, then your 2nd act break on another. Then your block comedy scene idea on another card. Then your climax/resolution. These are the main stops on your trip – the places you must get to along the way to make sure you stay on course. Do the same for your B-story.

After that, you can start adding scene ideas as they come to you. Don't worry if they're in the right order – this is just brainstorming time. Whenever you have another idea for another scene, move it to a new card.

Jack's Office

- **Liz returns from hiatus**
- **Jack tells Liz about SeinfeldVision**
- **Jerry's in Europe - doesn't know**
- **Quick cuts of Jerry in NBC shows (Law&Order, Heroes, Deal or No Deal)**

When you get stuck on one card, go to a new one. Think of an idea for a previous scene? Go back to that card and add it. Think you'll want a Writers' Room scene for the Jenna story but not sure what beats will go there? Just create a "Writers' Room" card as a placeholder. You'll add to it later or toss it if it isn't necessary.

Keep thinking of new scenes and beats and filling out cards. Add dialogue if you want. Use the back if you need to. If one card gets filled up front and back, you probably have too much in that scene. So, break it into two scenes on two cards.

The advantage of the card system is that you can shuffle the order of scenes easily and can run through your entire A-Story, then your B-story and C-stories, and then intersperse them as you like. Some writers like to lay out the cards on the floor so they can see the scene flow. Some pin them in order on a cork board. Whatever works for you.

If the ideas are really coming, you'll soon be adding bits of dialog, even squeezing your notes into the margins. The cards may begin to look messy but that's okay as long as you can read it.

Eventually you'll transfer your pile of cards to a typed version of the beat sheet, and that's what you'll be handing in.

More on C-stories

At this point, let's take a closer look at C-stories/runners. A common question is: what's the difference between a B-story and a C-story? The answer is, sometimes the difference is in the eye of the beholder.

Generally, a C-story gets less airtime and doesn't have to have a middle or end. It can just be a series of related scenes interspersed through the script that are there mostly for laughs.

The other big difference is, C-stories rarely have a large emotional impact on the characters. It would be unusual to see a C-story in one episode that changes the way the character(s) look at the world or live their lives in future episodes. In other words, they are generally one-offs – they're to fill out the episode but not to advance the season or series arc. They very rarely pay off down the line. (Unless you have a very cagey showrunner who is playing with the art form to throw off the audience's expectations.)

Whether the series you're writing uses an A/B/C structure or A/B/B or A/B/C/C is really, at some point, a subjective and semantic difference. The viewer and casual script reader won't care whether the writer thought it was a B-story or a C-runner. They'll just care whether they liked it or not.

For writers, C-runners often grow out of funny ideas that they simply couldn't build out into a beginning-middle-end, or just something to service the regulars that are light in the main plots. (On _30 Rock_, Jenna and Kenneth often show up in runners.)

Because they don't need to conform to the hard rules of storytelling, runners can be goofy or even surreal. And because of that, they can make a script with a more traditional A-story really memorable. So, my advice is to have fun with your runners and go *big funny*. It may end up being the part of the script you enjoy writing the most, and the part the audience remembers forever.

Remember the *Seinfeld* episode where a very attractive woman Jerry once dated shows up in his life again, but he cannot recall her first name? All he remembers is that it rhymed with a female body part. But she's super hot and he wants to date her again, so he tries all sorts of ways to trick her into mentioning her own name: introducing her to friends hoping she'll say it; making up childhood stories about getting teased about his own first name; brainstorming with George about possible names. ("Mulva"?) Finally, she realizes what's going on and angrily insists that Jerry say her name out loud. He can't, and she storms out of his apartment. Suddenly, Jerry has a realization: it's "Dolores."

That memorable storyline was just a series of beats about trying to remember an unusual name. It had no real payoff; Jerry's future was not terribly worse for having the woman storm out of his life. It's just a set-up, several funny scenes of him trying to remember the name, and the ending that it finally comes back to him but too late. The pun joke that the name "Dolores" rhymes with a certain intimate female body part is the big payoff of the story.

That's a classic example of a C-runner. A set-up (problem), an obstacle (he doesn't want her to know he forgot her name), lots of funny gags (beats) trying to solve the problem, and a jokey payoff that doesn't change anything.

The Written Beat Sheet

Some writers prefer to start their beat sheet at the keyboard, and that's okay too. It works just the same – start with a scene location and then bullet out the beats as you think of them.

So, the beat sheet scene for the first scene of the Tracy-Kenneth story might be:

STUDIO BACKSTAGE

- TRACY MOVING HIS STUFF INTO STUDIO KITCHEN
- LIZ LEARNS TRACY'S WIFE KICKED HIM OUT FOR "MINISTERING" TO A TRANSVESTITE PROSTITUTE
- TRACY IS NERVOUS - WHO'LL COOK FOR HIM AND TAKE CARE OF HIM?
- LIZ APPOINTS KENNETH TO BE TRACY'S OFFICE WIFE

And the first scene of the Jenna story might look like this:

MAKE-UP ROOM

- LIZ ASKS JENNA ABOUT HER SUMMER HIATUS
- JENNA STARRED IN A PLAY — "MYSTIC PIZZA: THE MUSICAL"
- LIZ NOTICES THAT JENNA'S PUT ON A TON OF WEIGHT
- JENNA SAYS IT'S BECAUSE SHE HAD TO EAT 4 SLICES OF PIZZA IN EVERY SHOW…32 SLICES A WEEK!
- JACK NOTICES JENNA'S WEIGHT GAIN
- LIZ PROMISES TO HELP HER SLIM BACK DOWN

Move things around, vamp, be creative. If you think of a great line or gag, jot it down. But mostly you want to beat out your story.

Not everything has to be in a beat sheet – not every scene, nor every entrance/exit. Later in the process, when you're outlining or writing, you may think of a scene that you need which never occurred to you before. That's okay. For now, you're just building the frame of the house. Don't worry about the wallpaper or the furniture – that comes much later.

Again, at this point, don't worry too much about the order of scenes. You can write each story out alone and then cut and paste them together, or just drop in scenes where you think they'll go and move them around until it feels right.

The full beat sheet should be about 3-6 pages single spaced. I'd like you to bring yours in around 3 pages. You can build a fuller version for yourself if you like, but I want your submission to hold at 3. We just want the raw bones of your story.

When you move to the outline, you'll have another chance to rearrange scenes and add some that you suddenly realize you need. (That often happens with transition scenes.) Keep adding and shuffling and filling in details until you think you've got the story pretty much beat out. Then re-read it to see if it will make sense to other people after they've read your logline.

If you think it makes general sense and lays out smoothly over two (or three) more or less equal acts, boom! – your beat sheet is done...for now.

ASSIGNMENT

WATCH – *ORDINARY PEOPLE, GOOD WILL HUNTING,* OR AN EPISODE OF *THE SOPRANOS* (WITH DR. MELFI) TO SEE HOW TO WRITE A GREAT THERAPY SCENE. (FOR YOUR THERAPIST COUCH EXERCISE.) THEY'RE ALSO GREAT EXAMPLES OF TOP-NOTCH WRITING.

READ – THE *EPISODES* BEAT SHEET POSTED ON HTTPS://KEVINKEL TON.COM/LINKS. (WRITTEN BY A TALENTED FORMER STUDENT OF MINE, MARCHAND STORCH. IT STANDS AS ONE OF THE BEST I'VE READ.)

WRITE – A 3 PAGE BEAT SHEET FOR YOUR EPISODE (8-12 SCENES FOR A 4-CAMERA TAPE SHOW OR 12-20 SCENES FOR A FILM SHOW) THAT TELLS YOUR STORY, INCLUDING SCENE LOCATION, INCITING INCIDENT, MAJOR PLOT POINTS, AND BLOCK COMEDY SCENE(S).

4

INGREDIENTS: FINDING CHARACTERS

INGREDIENTS:
-FIND A PROTOTYPE
-EXPLORE THEIR BACKGROUND AND PSYCHE
-ADD QUIRKS
-SEASON WITH NEUROSES AND FLAWS

Okay, so let's say you have an idea for your character - maybe you wrote a bio or found a prototype - but you will want to get deeper. Here are two writing exercises that will help you find the character and maybe come up with some cool material you'll end up using in your script.

The Therapist Couch
Write a scene in which you put your character into counseling/therapy.

You be the therapist - or choose a fictional therapist - and put your character through the process. Write a session or several sessions worth. Make her really dig deep into her past or her psyche for why she behaves the way she does or makes the choices she's going to make in your script. Why are her actions so different from her stated believes or normal morality? What would his father think about his choices? His mother? What happened in his/her past to create the series of choices she'll ultimately make in your story?

You know what writer does this a lot? Woody Allen. Go re-watch *Annie Hall, Bananas* or *Take the Money and Run.* Woody loves to put his characters on the couch. In *Crimes and Misdemeanors,* it's someone talking to their rabbi, but it's essentially the same device. He uses the therapy sessions to tell and advance his stories and let the audience inside the characters' heads. So does *Prince of Tides, Good Will Hunting* and *Ordinary People.* (And many other movies.)

You may not want to use therapy scenes in your script, but the time your character spends in therapy will not be wasted.

Date Your Character

That's right, sit down and write a first date for your character to go on. Have him/her go out with you, or even better, with another famous fictional character - maybe Annie Hall or Benjamin Braddock (*The Graduate*), or with whomever you think they'd mix well.

Let their date banter be the road to learning about them, how they see themself, and how their date will perceive them. How do they treat the hostess and waiters? Are they honest? What are they willing to reveal to their date, and to themselves?

This is a great way to establish who your character is at the beginning of your script. It may be at odds with how they react to plot points and who they ultimately prove to be. That's a GOOD thing. You want a complex character who is different (usually better) than who they thought they were. You want someone who will rise to the occasion.

But by taking your character on a date or two, you will establish a starting point for who they are and where they've been. And who knows, some of that date dialogue might just end up in your final draft.

You can also place your characters in a stressful environment – in a stuck elevator, at a craps table in Las Vegas, waiting in line at the DMV. Be creative. Put them under pressure. It could be time pressure, money pressure, social pressure. Then see how they react. It's much more fun than writing bios, and I bet you'll learn more about your characters than any long-winded, painfully detailed bio you can dream up.

ASSIGNMENT

READ – THE *PARKS AND RECREATION* BEAT SHEET (WRITTEN BY ANOTHER EXCELLENT FORMER STUDENT OF MINE, RYAN GRASHOW) IN THE RESOURCES SECTION.

WATCH - ANOTHER EPISODE (OR TWO...OR MORE) OF THE SERIES YOU'VE CHOSEN TO SPEC. YOU HAVE TO REALLY KNOW A SERIES BEFORE YOU CAN DUPLICATE ITS STYLE AND TONE.

WRITE – A SCENE PLACING ONE OR TWO OF YOUR CHARACTERS IN AN AWKWARD SITUATION. *THIS IS A WRITING EXERCISE AND WILL NOT BE IN YOUR SCRIPT.* YOU CAN SET IT DURING THE TIMELINE OF YOUR SCRIPT, OR AT SOME TIME BEFORE YOUR STORY BEGINS OR AFTER IT ENDS. MAKE FUN CHOICES.

5

WHAT MAKES A GOOD STORY?

INGREDIENTS:
-INCITING INCIDENT
-GOALS/WANTS/NEEDS
-CONFLICT
-OBSTACLES AND TWISTS
-ESCALATED CONFLICT
-ADDITIONAL OBSTACLES AND TWISTS (ADD TO TASTE)
-SATISFYING CONCLUSION

Students sometimes ask me for a more in-depth look at what makes a good sitcom episode and story. Though I see this book more as a writing workshop than a sitcom theory course, I think the request is reasonable. So, let's look at that question.

First off, I want to reiterate that the proper question isn't: "What makes a good sitcom story?" It's: "What makes a good story?" Sitcoms follow the very same rules of drama as any other story-driven art form. Make it compelling, clever, original, and satisfying. I don't care whether you're writing a 5-act play, *Two Broke Girls*, or a segment of *60 Minutes* - those rules are universal and immutable. 'Nuff said.

Now let's look at *how* we accomplish that.

Sitcoms Are Charactercoms

To begin, let's understand that sitcoms are really all about characters. In fact, they shouldn't be called situation comedies at all - they are character comedies.

Pretty much all comedy comes from character. And the more interesting the character, the more potential for interesting comedy. That's why good TV characters are so very quirky – it makes them more interesting than real people, and hence more likely to react to normal situations with funny responses.

Example 1:

George Costanza of *Seinfeld* is quirkier and more interesting than me. When I leave a rambling, embarrassing message on a girl's voice mail, I simply fret over it. When George leaves an embarrassing voice message, he breaks into the girl's apartment to steal the tape.

In dramatic terms, George and I are both in conflict with a girl we like. My response to that conflict is internal, expected, and hence not very interesting. George's is external and unique – but very logical and creative when you think about it – hence it's funny.

In the movie *Swingers,* Michael has the same problem but a different response: he keeps calling the girl back, leaving even more embarrassing messages. He can't stop. Different reactions, both funny.

Example 2:

Lots of 40ish single women I know want to be married. Most of them grouse about it internally. Liz Lemon buys a wedding dress and wears it to work. Same conflict, different responses. If your real-life gal pal did that, you'd worry she needs major psycholog-ical intervention. When Liz does it, you laugh.

Why is Liz doing it funny, but your best friend doing it is not? Because you don't worry about Liz, because you know she's not real and you don't care about her mental health.

Creating Conflict

To create conflict, you simply give the character a want or need and then make them do stuff to achieve it that no one else would do.

Or you make their situation exaggeratedly awkward and uncomfortable. If the situation is big, their reaction can be small and typical. It's still funny because of the dissonance between the size of the conflict and the subtlety of their response.

In other words, mismatch the size of the problem with the size of the response. George Costanza had a relatively small problem (embarrassment) and chose a ridiculously large response (breaking and entering).

Or Vice President of the United States Selena Meyer can have a big problem (her clean jobs task force program is imploding) and chose a small response (going to a yogurt shop to get good PR).

So, if you are stuck with how to start or advance your story, think about what can go wrong for the character, or what they can do that is an overreaction to a simple problem.

Okay, so that's how to create conflict. But you kind of knew that already. Now the question becomes: how do you apply that in the sitcom structure?

Character Dynamics

Here's a very basic paradigm for half-hour comedy (courtesy of Dan Harmon, creator of *Community*):

1. A character is in a zone of comfort
2. But they want something
3. The character enters an unfamiliar or uncomfortable situation to seek that something
4. They are forced to adapt (Often, while trying to adapt, things get worse)
5. They pay a heavy price for their actions
6. They ultimately get what they want or give up trying
7. Because it's a continuing TV series, they return to their familiar comfort zone
8. But in some small way, they've changed or grown as a person (or become a worse version of their earlier self)

That's pretty much it. Your job is to take the character out of her comfort zone and then make them pay a heavy price for their actions. Without killing them.

So, in our sample script, "SeinfeldVision":

1. Jack is in his comfort zone, running NBC
2. Jack wants something: higher ratings.
3. To get them, he enters an uncomfortable zone: he steals/misuses Jerry Seinfeld's image. (I'd argue that Jack knew it was not right even though he bragged about it to Liz.) Jerry finds out.
4. Jack is forced to adapt: hide from Jerry in his (Jack's) own kingdom, 30 Rock

5. Jack pays a heavy price: anxiety, legal jeopardy, humiliation, paying Jerry for his sins
6. Jack gets what he wants: use of Jerry's image and potentially higher ratings
7. Jack returns to his familiar comfort zone: safe in his NBC job
8. Jack has changed/grown: he's giving money to charity that he otherwise hadn't planned on

Is all character comedy rooted in conflict?

Yes and no. A lot of comedy, especially TV comedy, comes out of personal awkwardness. Social awkwardness is an *internal conflict*. (As are insecurities, neuroses, and feelings of inadequacy.)

We rarely laugh when people are in real, life-threatening conflict. (Unless it's over-the-top and hence not real.) You don't laugh at *Reservoir Dogs* (well, most of us don't) but you do laugh at *Django Unchained*, because the second is cartoonish violent conflict. Same is true for *Pulp Fiction* - Tarantino makes the violence just cartoony or ironic enough that we don't take it seriously, so we can laugh at it.

But conflict that can be resolved and isn't threatening can be funny. Archie Bunker's bigotry is funny because we know he's never going to don a white hood and hurt anyone. Some people even laugh at Sean Hannity or Rachel Maddow for the same reason. (Had to be non-partisan there.)

No one gets hurt when someone feels awkward, but we are happy it isn't us. I think the laugh it invokes, on some subconscious level, is how we cope with the fact that we are happy it's them, not us. Eight hundred years ago, people watched gladiators get mauled by lions and enjoyed it because, thank God, it wasn't *them*. Same with stonings. But now we just watch Ted Lasso say awkward things. No blood, same result.

So, when you are looking for a comedy beat, ask yourself: how you can make the character feel awkward or embarrassed?

Writing Jokes

There are many types of humor, so there can be no one definition. What makes a great line funny has nothing to do with what makes a sight gag or physical comedy funny.

But to generalize about wit, a funny line is simply a new way of thinking that the audience hadn't considered yet. They laugh at the realization of that new logic.

> "SOME GUY HIT MY CAR FENDER THE OTHER DAY, AND I SAID UNTO HIM, 'BE FRUITFUL AND MULTIPLY.' BUT NOT IN THOSE WORDS."
> —WOODY ALLEN

It's funny because when we hear it and realize, for the first time, that saying F--- Y-- is essentially the same as saying "be fruitful and multiply." But one is biblical and loving, and the other is New Yorker and hostile.

It also highlights dissonance – a conflict or incongruence in the character's thinking or response to a situation. Allen didn't want to tell you what he actually said (in reaction to his conflict), so he replaced his vulgarism with a biblical quote.

Humor is rooted in conflict. It's the proton of storytelling. Go listen to any stand-up, and I'll bet 90% of what they say (their premises) are rooted in some kind of conflict. Be it dating, or parents, or bosses, or weird observations about life. Their character has a conflict, and they resolve it in a clever and compelling way that you never would have thought of yourself.

So, when you are stuck on coming up with a funny line, just write a typical line that anyone might say, then look at it and ask yourself, "How can I say/convey that same thought in a different logic?" How can you say it sarcastically? Dimwittedly? Naively?

Ironically? How can you get from point A to D, without going through B and C? How can you go A-C-B-D instead of A-B-C-D?

Let me re-emphasize: a witty or funny line is just applying fresh logic to an old thought.

> "THIS IS NOT A NOVEL TO BE TOSSED ASIDE LIGHTLY. IT SHOULD BE THROWN WITH GREAT FORCE."
>
> "DON'T LOOK AT ME IN THAT TONE OF VOICE."
>
> "TELL HIM I WAS TOO FUCKING BUSY -- OR VICE VERSA."
>
> "BEAUTY IS ONLY SKIN DEEP, BUT UGLY GOES CLEAN TO THE BONE."
>
> — ALL BY DOROTHY PARKER

So, whenever you are stuck on a scene or a joke, ask yourself, "what's the conflict here? What potential conflict can I insert here? How do I make things *uncomfortable* for this character?" Because when someone else is uncomfortable, we find it funny. (Probably because, thank God, it's not happening to us!) It's just human nature.

Okay, now how do I DO all that?

Trial and error.

I could be glib and leave it at that. Because I believe that writing is 50% innate talent and 50% working hard at it. But you deserve the best answer I can give you, so I'll try.

You compile scenes, bits, gags, and jokes. You do it by thinking a lot. You watch tons of half hour comedies (or immerse yourself in whatever form you're writing). You analyze what you watch. You apply those insights to your work. If the show you're writing has lots of short scenes, you write lots of short scenes. If the show has broad physical comedy bits, you come up with some broad physical bits. You start to put them in order and move them around, always using your story as the spine on which to hang bits, gags, and lines of dialogue. You keep asking yourself:

- "Would this character do/say this?"
- "Am I revealing the character or contradicting him?"
- "Is what she is doing in this situation logical in her world?"
- "Is what I'm making him do interesting to me, and will it be interesting to lots of other people?"
- "Will putting this on paper amuse readers and make them think I can write other sitcoms?"

That's the only formula I know. I'm sure there are story gurus out there that can break it down into a formula or detailed steps – put this kind of scene here, that kind of reaction there, make sure you have three of these in act one and six of those in act two. But the truth is, those are just guidelines.

Long before *Seinfeld*, I once asked Larry David if he'd ever read any screenwriting books. He said no, because he didn't want to adopt any "rules" that would make him write like other people. He wanted to be original. And I'd say, he was.

There are no rules or easy formulas to TV writing success. If there were, everyone would quit their McDonalds jobs and become a story editor on *The Simpsons*. But 99.99999% of them can't.

The ones who could, sat down and figured out for themselves how to tell a great story using those characters. They were in conflict – they wanted to be highly paid TV writers.

But unlike most normal people, they did something unique and compelling: they sat down and wrote a great script. (And probably a few not-so-great ones first.)

The moral: be unique and compelling. Don't grouse about being single. Wear the wedding dress. Write the great script...or at least try damn hard. Leave your comfort zone. (Which you've already done by reading this book.) Adapt and pay the heavy price. (Which you're doing by working hard on your story and script.)

By the end of your personal third act, it may just pay off.

ASSIGNMENT

READ – THE *HOW I MET YOUR MOTHER* OUTLINE (WRITTEN BY CHUCK TATHAM) POSTED AT HTTPS://KEVINKELTON.COM/LINKS

WRITE — CONTINUE TO REFINE AND ADD BEATS TO YOUR BEAT SHEET.

6

THE OUTLINE

INGREDIENTS:

-1 THEME (WRITTEN AS A SINGLE SENTENCE OR QUESTION)

-3 TO 4 STORYLINES (A/B/C/D)

-3 TO 4 LEAD CHARACTERS (ONE FOR EACH STORY)

-COLD OPEN (OR TEASER) PLUS 2 OR 3 ACTS

-12 TO 20 SCENES WITH SLUGLINES

-BEATS AND JOKES (ADD LIBERALLY)

By now you've got a beat sheet and hopefully used some of our feedback to refine it. Now you start turning it into an outline. And here's the good news: you don't need to start from scratch. You're simply going to build your outline from inside your beat sheet.

This is a simple process that *I think* I invented. Who knows, maybe someone else does it this way, too. Either way, it works. And if you use this process, you'll never have to face a blank page again—at least until you begin your next spec script.

Sluglines

This is where you begin to learn the jargon of teleplays and screenplays.

The first thing you're going to do is turn your sets/locations into sluglines. If you don't know what a slugline is, go to the sample outlines at the end of this book. A slugline tells the reader where a scene takes place – INT. for interior scenes and EXT. for exteriors – the exact location, and whether it takes place in DAY or NIGHT.

When you finally get to writing your outline (and script), the set location will be part of your slugline - the line that starts every scene in a script. It usually looks like this...

EXT. 30 ROCKEFELLER PLAZA - MORNING

Or...

INT. JACK'S OFFICE - DAY

Part of your assignment this time is to review the "Formatting for Half-Hour Shows" document about sitcom script formatting and terminology. (Posted at HTTPS://KEVINKELTON.COM/LINKS)

You don't need to learn it all now, but glance through it. You'll see a detailed explanation of sluglines and other important script terms that you'll need later.

Outlining Scenes

Once you have all your sluglines in place, go to the first scene of your beat sheet and simply start turning bullets into complete sentences. This is where you write your story in paragraph form. So, this....

STUDIO BACK STAGE

- TRACY MOVING HIS STUFF INTO STUDIO KITCHEN
- LIZ LEARNS TRACY'S WIFE KICKED HIM OUT FOR "MINISTERING" TO A TRANSVESTITE PROSTITUTE
- TRACY IS NERVOUS - WHO'LL COOK FOR HIM AND TAKE CARE OF HIM?
- LIZ APPOINTS KENNETH TO BE TRACY'S OFFICE WIFE

...becomes...

INT. STUDIO BACK STAGE - MOMENTS LATER

LIZ SPOTS DOTCOM AND TRACY MOVING TRACY'S LUGGAGE AND BELONGINGS INTO HIS DRESSING ROOM. TRACY TELLS KENNETH HE'S GOING TO BE USING THE BACKSTAGE KITCHEN AREA AS HIS NEW BATHROOM, "SO SPREAD THE WORD." LIZ ASKS WHAT'S GOING ON AND LEARNS THAT TRACY'S WIFE KICKED HIM OUT FOR "MINISTERING" TO A TRANSVESTITE PROSTITUTE. DOTCOM: "HE DOESN'T MESS WITH THEM - HE JUST TRIES TO GET THEM INTO COMPUTER SCHOOL." BUT IT TURNS OUT THAT A PAPARAZZI SNAPPED A PHOTO OF TRACY WITH THE PROSTITUTE AND ANGIE SAW IT IN THE TABLOIDS, SO NOW HE'S A MAN WITHOUT A HOME.

LIZ TELLS HIM TO GO HOME AND APOLOGIZE TO ANGIE BUT TRACY REFUSES, SINCE THIS IS THE FIRST TIME IN HIS LIFE, HE DIDN'T DO ANYTHING WRONG. BUT TRACY IS NERVOUS - WHO'LL DO HIS ONLINE BANKING, WRITE HIS BLOG, AND DO THE COOKING ON TACO WEDNESDAYS? LIZ, IN A RUSH TO GET OUT OF THERE, APPOINTS KENNETH TO BE TRACY'S "OFFICE WIFE." TRACY LOVES THE IDEA. HE GETS DOWN ON ONE KNEE, PULLS A RING OUT OF HIS POCKET, AND ASKS KENNETH TO "TAKE THIS RING, SELL IT IN THE JEWISH PART OF MIDTOWN, AND USE THE MONEY TO BUY US A NINTENDO WII." KENNETH: "YES, YES, A THOUSAND TIMES, YES!"

Of course, I had the slight advantage of being able to read the actual script and parse it down into what the outline might have looked like. Maybe it wasn't that close to how the actual scene played out, but this is what a sitcom scene should generally look like in outline form.

You don't need as many specific jokes as this sample shows. Some writers like to add a few at this stage if they have them, other writers prefer to just write the basic story beats. I suggest you try to add at least one joke in every scene of your outline unless it's a very short scene. It always helps to have a laugh or two in there when someone's reading it.

Now repeat that process with every scene, and (you guessed it) – boom! – you've got an outline.

Staff written outlines tend to be much more detailed and can run upward of 8-12 pages or more. But for our purposes, let's keep it a little more basic and not go over 6 pages. *Yes, I said SIX.* Brevity is the soul of wit. And the soul of an outline.

Cold Openings, Acts and Tags

As your outline starts to take shape, you'll start laying your scenes into acts.

The number of acts depends on the series you're writing. A *30 Rock* episode uses a three-act structure, with a Cold Opening leading into the opening titles, then flows right into the show's first act. *But their scripts start at the beginning of Act One, and they create the Cold Opening in editing.*

So, you have to read scripts for your show and see how they *write it* – not how it looks on air. Sorry, I know it's hard to track down scripts, but that's the way the game is played.

Some shows use a prologue and two acts (it's really three acts, but that's how they name them). Some shows use a short cold opening (2-3 pages) that lead into titles, then go to commercial, and then two acts. And some shows include a tag that plays during the closing credits.

Figure out what structure your show uses and follow it exactly. If you don't use their structure and format, I can guarantee you they will not use your script.

Pacing Your Story

As you write the outline, you should have a sense of how your story is playing, in both screen time and in pace. You want to follow long scenes with shorter scenes and vary the length of scenes to keep things moving. In the older sitcoms of the '70s and '80s, when most sitcoms were shot in a studio in front of a live audience, the stage space was limited and shows usually had only 4-5 sets per episode. That meant writing longer, block style scenes – sometimes only 3 to an act. (*All In The Family* sometimes ran an entire act in one scene.)

But as shows like *Seinfeld* became more sophisticated at the end of the 80s, they moved out of the studio and started interspersing exterior scenes. They also morphed to a more rapid, film style pace that used very short scenes (sometimes half or even a third of a page) and other filmic devices that made the story move more quickly. Now most series have at least 12 scenes in an episode and often many more. I counted thirty-three scenes in "*SienfeldVision.*"

So, watch several episodes of your series (and read a few of its scripts if you can find them) to see how they pace their stories. Then duplicate that pacing. While you want your script to stand out in terms of hook and comedy, you want to mimic their format and style EXACTLY. If your story doesn't feel like a typical story for that series, it will be dismissed no matter how smart or funny it is. And it will not only be dismissed by that series, but it will be dismissed by every knowledgable agent, studio or network exec who opens it, too.

That said, go forth, my children, and multiply your beat sheet into an outline. Simple, right? (Hint: The answer is, "Yes, Kevin. Yes, it is.")

What is Story Structure?

Ah...the eternal question of a writer's life! As ten writers, you'll get ten different answers. And most of them will have published a book on theirs.

You can read dozens of writing books and study a gazillion screenplay gurus, and they will all have their own terminology and philosophy. I'm no different.

So, here's what I think is the classic story structure, no matter whether you're writing a half-hour sitcom, a one-hour drama, a screenplay or a play.

The 3-Act Story Paradigm

What is structure? It's beginning, middle, and end. Yep, it's that simple. Just make sure your story has an inciting incident, a series of complications, twists, obstacles, escalations, a crisis, a climax, and a resolution. Hit those milestones with rising tension and some snappy dialogue and visuals, and you've got a story.

ASSIGNMENT

REVIEW – THE FORMATTING FOR HALF-HOUR SHOWS DOCUMENT AT HTTPS://KEVINKELTON.COM/LINKS

READ – THE SPEC *PEN15* OUTLINE EXCERPT IN THE RESOURCES SECTION (WRITTEN BY A VERY TALENTED FORMER STUDENT OF MINE, AMANDA MAISONAVE).

WATCH – MORE EPISODES OF YOUR SERIES.

WRITE – ONE SCENE FROM YOUR STORY IN OUTLINE FORM WITH SLUGLINE, ACTION AND STORY BEATS, AND SNIPPETS OF DIALOGUE.

7

DIALOGUE AND JOKES

Spicing Things Up

INGREDIENTS:
-RHYTHM AND PACING
-WORD CHOICE
-SURPRISE
-TIMING (BROUGHT BY ACTORS, DIRECTORS AND EDITORS)

To be painfully honest, there's only so much anyone can teach you about dialogue. Most people can either write it or they can't. But I'll share some rules and tricks with you that may help you hone this innate skill on your own.

First of all, to really learn to write dialog, you have to **read dialogue.** Reading scripts is an absolute must. You will never understand dialogue until you see it in printed form and "speak" textual dialogue like it's a second language.

So, the first thing to do is get your hand on good scripts – as many as possible – and start reading and studying what good dialogue looks like. TV scripts, movie scripts, and plays. Read David Mamet plays. Read *On Golden Pond*. Read

The Office or old *Mad About You* scripts. I particularly liked reading *Mad About You* scripts because they were so conversational and lean.

What you should see in great dialogue scripts is that the dialogue "bounces" – meaning most lines are just that, one line long. Maybe a line and a half. But you will rarely see paragraphs of dialogue coming from one person at one time.

As a young writer I developed a bizarre skill that I think really helped me, and I highly suggest you try to develop as well. After reading a ton of movie scripts, when I went to the movies, I would watch the movie but SEE THE SCRIPT in my mind. I visualized the page floating in front of me, hear the dialogue and imagine what it must have looked like on the page. How long the line looked. How it might have been punctuated. Was that stutter in the script? Did the writer use a en dash or an ellipse for that pause? I trained myself to "see" the dialogue that I heard. Then, when I was writing dialogue of my own, I could compare it to the great movie dialogue I'd "seen" before.

Try it. It takes a while to get it down, and if you do develop the habit, it may ruin a few movies for you. As you'll be more transfixed on the script in your head than on the movie you paid $11 to see. But you'll be "writing in your head" – and writing good stuff, because it's already been written and produced by the top players in Hollywood.

The look of Good Dialogue

Good dialogue doesn't look like a sentence. It looks like a sentence fragment. Sometimes just a word or two.

Most people don't talk in sentences. They just don't. When you're out with friends or in a restaurant, listen to the conversations around you. Again, see them on the script page in your head. Even create the Slugline. See real life as a script!

```
INT. PANERA BREAD COFFEE SHOP - LATE MORNING

Kevin sits at a table in the back, banging out
his writing lesson on his trusty MacBook Pro. He
as he types, he begins eavesdropping on two women
in a nearby booth.

                  BLONDE LADY
        These are the photos--

                  PIGTAIL FRIEND
        All of them?

                  BLONDE LADY
        Uh, most. Jerry's in blue.

                  PIGTAIL FRIEND
        Okay--
```

I won't go on, since it's a pretty boring conversation. But you get the point. People talk in short, clipped phrases without perfect transitions or connections. When you write dialog, write the way people speak, then go back and see if it reads well. You may overdo the "heys" and "uhs" at first, so go back and trim them out. Most of those are acting interpretations that don't belong on the page. But if they are absolutely necessary to sound right, put it in.

Of course, a sitcom script has to be tight, so you can't get too naturalistic. There's a happy medium, and it will come to you as you study good scripts and play with the dialogue you write. If you're writing too much chuffa and going too long between laughs or story points, go in and tighten it.

What Makes a Great Joke?

Simple – a great joke is a funny thing someone says when the person saying it *doesn't know it's funny*.

This is a very difficult rule to follow when writing a sitcom, where there is so much emphasis on keeping the laughs going. Too often sitcoms are populated by characters that are supposed to be unusually witty, like Frasier and Niles, who walk around all day saying funny things on purpose.

But few real people have that skill. And a great character rarely does. So, when you read a comedy script, every time you come to a line that you think is funny (or that you think will elicit a laugh from the audience), ask yourself if the person saying it meant it to be funny or meant it to be serious. If they meant it seriously and it made you laugh, it's a great line. If they said it to be funny, well, it still may be a great joke, but it's not the highest form of the art of writing dialogue.

Here's an example from *Modern Family*. It's got two laugh lines in one speech – one that sounds like a joke, and one that doesn't.

JAY

You do realize that's a suicide mission, right? He's 13, he's in a new school, and if he declares his love for a 16 year-old girl while wearing a puffy-sleeved white shirt, we're going to be heading down to that school Monday morning with a bolt cutter to get him out of his locker.

(then noticing)

Oh geez, he's picking flowers.

The first laugh – the "bolt cutter" line – well, maybe Jay is knowingly trying to turn a clever phrase, maybe not. But it *sounds* like a joke. I particularly love the last line because Jay isn't saying it to be funny. Yet it's so in character and the rhythm is so perfect that it "pops" – we know it will be funny coming out of his mouth, even if he didn't say it to be funny.

The Element of Surprise

Often, surprise is the key to finding a laugh. Taking a normal thought and twisting it in a way the audience didn't anticipate. The line becomes funny not because it's an overt joke, but because something comes out of left field that the viewer didn't see coming.

> "WOULD I RATHER BE FEARED OR LOVED? EASY. BOTH. I WANT PEOPLE TO BE AFRAID OF HOW MUCH THEY LOVE ME."
> —MICHAEL SCOTT (THE OFFICE)

In that example, Michael Scott doesn't know he's saying something funny. He doesn't intend to. But the idea that he could conflate fear and love into one emotion is the surprise that makes us laugh.

Sometimes it's taking a clean thought that goes from A to B to C to D and rearranging it, or dropping out C completely. Or leaving off D and letting the audience fill it in on their own.

> "THAT'S PERFECT — BRIAN BEING A SEISMOLOGIST, AND YOU HAVING SO MANY FAULTS."
> — FRASIER

In that example, yes, Frasier is probably trying to be witty. But what makes the line work is the C thought that is left out:

A) YOU TWO ARE PERFECT TOGETHER BECAUSE...
B) HE IS A SEISMOLOGIST...
C) AND SEISMOLOGISTS STUDY EARTHQUAKE FAULT LINES...
D) AND YOU HAVE SO MANY FAULTS.

We reflexively fill in the necessary thoughts to make the line work, and then laugh because of what was missing.

When you break down humor this way, it can lose some of its magic, just like when you learn the secret behind a magic trick. But as writers, if we understand what makes a line of thought funny, we can take a normal sentence and reconstruct it into a line of dialogue that elicits a laugh.

That's the *trick* of joke construction.

Stylized Dialogue

Of course, every series has a different style – or "voice" – so dialogue that would be right for one may be wrong for another.

30 Rock dialogue is more stylized, with a longer and more convoluted sentence structure, whereas dialogue in *The Office* and *Modern Family* is more clipped and naturalistic.

The best way to test your dialogue is to read it out loud. Say it, don't just think it. You may want to read it aloud with a significant other or good friend. Someone you trust to have fun with it and not be judgmental. Or compare your scene to a scene from an actual script from the show to see if it looks the same on the page.

Of course, the humor will never be as sharp as hearing it come out of the actors who play the characters. But you need to develop a sense of what works for each actor and what will read like they speak.

And always remember, you are writing your spec script to be read, not performed. At this stage, it's more important it *reads* like a script for the show in the eyes of people who don't work for the show. That's a hard concept to grasp. Just remember, the odds of your script actually getting made by that show are very slim. But you want a script that other people think would make a good episode of the show. Those people – producers, agents, studio executives – will then consider you for other shows based on the strength of your sample script. Writers rarely get hired on the show they spec out. But a good spec for one show can open doors to assignments and staff jobs on other shows, and that's how most careers get started.

Doing the Grunt Work

Trying to write a working outline is probably the single toughest step of television writing.

If you are part of a TV staff that broke the story together and set you up with a dozen or so good jokes to use, you might be able to turn around a solid first draft outline in two or three days. But if you discover story problems or just can't get a handle on how to make this particular set of stories funny, it can be an agonizing process that lasts for a week or longer.

And again, that's if you have a staff to lean on. If you are writing your outline on spec, everything falls to you (and your partner if you have one.) Not to frighten you, but writing is supposed to be hard. As my first manager used to say, "If it was easy, they wouldn't need you."

When to Abandon the Outline

This is a tricky question.

A lot of it depends on if you're writing a spec script or you're being paid (for a freelance assignment or staff job). If it's for pay and your outline has been approved by the powers that be (the people paying you), they consider that outline a sort of contract. And they expect you to deliver on what was promised. If you get into story trouble on an approved outline, first try very hard to make the approved outline beats work. If you can't, call the producers and set up a meeting to discuss it. If they say, don't worry about the outline, just write what you think works, you have your answer.

This happened to me once when I was writing a freelance script for a new series being produced by the incredibly talented team of Lowell Ganz and Babaloo Mandel. We broke the story together, but when I went home to write it, I just couldn't make the last two scenes work. So, I called them to explain the story problem and say I have a fix I'd like to try. They trusted my judgment enough to say, "Sure, go for it." The first draft I turned in must have pleased them, because soon after they hired me to be on staff.

Other times the producers will call you back into their office to discuss the problem and try to make you see how the approved outline *can* work. Most producers will work with you to get an outline you can write, as long as you give them notice. What they don't like is unpleasant surprises when the first draft arrives and it's not what they were expecting.

But if you're writing on spec and the story doesn't seem to be working, well, there's no law that says you have to write an unworkable script. Stop, figure out a better way, outline it again, and let your imagination take the wheel. As long as the script turns out well, no one cares if you followed your outline or not. The danger, of course, is getting lost along the new path. But then, you can always return to your original story and outline. And maybe your brief detour will give you new insights into how to fix the original story.

ASSIGNMENT

READ – THE *30 ROCK* OUTLINE, "UNWINDULAX" (WRITTEN BY TINA FEY AND MATT HUBBARD) POSTED AT HTTPS://KEVINKEL TON.COM/LINKS

THAT IS THE FORMAT YOU SHOULD BE USING, THOUGH THIS OUTLINE USES A LOT MORE DIALOGUE THAN I WANT YOU TO USE

AT THIS POINT. NO MORE THAN TWO (2) JOKES OF DIALOGUE PER
SCENE.

WRITE – COMPLETE A ROUGH DRAFT OF YOUR FULL OUTLINE.

COLLABORATE - IF YOU CAN, FIND A FUNNY OR CREATIVE
FRIEND TO READ YOUR OUTLINE AND SEE IF YOU CAN COLLABO-
RATE WITH THEM TO ADD 1-2 JOKES TO EACH SCENE (OR AS
MANY SCENES AS POSSIBLE).

SOPHISTICATED STRUCTURES

INGREDIENTS:
-ONE STORY IDEA WITH A THEME, INCITING INCIDENT,
AND A BEGINNING, MIDDLE AND ENDING
-WORKABLE A/B/C STORIES
-SPICE WITH MORE SUB-STORYLINES AND MORE
COMPLEXITIES, TRYING TO TIE THEM TOGETHER INTO A
COHESIVE WHOLE

As I noted previously, more and more series these days are chucking the traditional A/B/C storytelling style for more sophisticated story structures. In shows on HBO, Netflix, Apple TV, and other newer platforms, show creators are crafting episode arcs that involve multiple plots interwoven more like a movie than a half-hour sitcom. Let's look at one of those series.

A Look At "Veep"

In recent years half-hour comedies on cable and streaming platforms have gotten more and more sophisticated in both their humor and storytelling.

Let's analyze the structure of an episode of the HBO series *Veep* titled *"Catherine."*

You can view the entire episode here. Or you may read a written synopsis of the episode here.

I chose this episode to study because it uses a very sophisticated story structure. Also, because premium cable series do not have commercials, some writers assume they don't have act breaks. But that is a mistaken assumption. Every well-crafted story has at least one act break. Some half-hour stories use a three-act structure with two breaks (similar to movie structure). Finding the act breaks can be tricky without the help of commercials but trust me, they are there.

The Logline

Here is the *TV Guide* logline for the episode:

> SELINA AND HER DAUGHTER CLASH OVER THE CHOICE OF A FAMILY DOG.

Here's the HBO logline:

> FACED WITH A TRUMPED-UP STORY OF A RIFT BETWEEN THE VEEP AND THE FIRST LADY, SELINA QUELLS ACCUSATIONS THAT EVERYTHING IS ABOUT HER--EVEN THOUGH IT IS. THE VEEP'S OFFICE GOES INTO SPIN CONTROL ABOUT THE APPOINTMENT OF AN 'OIL GUY' TO THE CLEAN JOBS TASK FORCE. GARY SELECTS CANDIDATES FOR THE VP DOG, THOUGH SELINA'S DAUGHTER CATHERINE, WHO IS VISITING FROM COLLEGE, HAS FINAL SAY.

And here is a fan site logline:

> SELINA TRIES TO PROVE SHE IS NOT AN EGOMANIAC BY IMPROVING
> HER RELATIONSHIP WITH HER DAUGHTER, WHILE ALSO FENDING
> OFF RUMORS ABOUT AN ALLEGED FALLING-OUT WITH THE PRESI-
> DENT'S WIFE. HOWEVER, HER TEAM IS FRANTICALLY TRYING TO
> CONTROL THE LATEST CONTROVERSY ABOUT THE CLEAN JOBS TASK
> FORCE, AND ANOTHER PROBLEM FLARES UP WHEN A LIST OF POTEN-
> TIAL NAMES FOR HURRICANES IS ISSUED.

Notice how each logline leads with a different take on the main plot. (Interestingly, only the fan site gets it right in terms of which is the A-story.) As you'll come to see, people who write TV loglines don't know bupkis about story. They're not professional script writers and they write the logline to highlight what they think are the most promotable hooks. But that may not be what the story is really about.

Analyzing the Structure

The script for *"Catherine"* uses a sophisticated structure of dual, "competing A-stories."

One A-story is about Selina's need to get a senator's approval for a key appointment to a White House task force, and the other A-story is about Selina's need to bond with her daughter. In this episode she is torn between two competing needs – to advance her career or to improve her personal relationships – and only one will win out.

But that's not why they are called "competing A-stories." These are competing main plots because they carry about equal weight in screen time and in emotional impact on Selina. Some writers might argue that it's really just an A/B structure with a "heavy" B-story, meaning it has almost equal screen time and importance.

Whether the structure is A/A or A/B is purely academic – it won't affect how funny the script is or whether the episode wins an Emmy.

But as writers it's important to us because it helps us analyze the complexities of half-hour storytelling and hopefully be able to tell better stories in our own scripts.

So, for learning purposes we'll call it an A/A structure with two stories of more or less equal importance. One is important to Selina's career, the other to her personal life. Having one character drive competing A-stories is very tricky, and this script pulls it off extremely well.

The episode also has three B-stories:

1. Selina's rift with the First Lady, who thinks Selina is a diva.
2. Selina's name being used for a hurricane.
3. Selina's 20-year anniversary in Washington politics.

The episode also has three C-runners:

1. Mike's fake dog.
2. Jonah's pathetic attempts to score with women.
3. Gary's role as Selina's factoid man.

These are runners because they have no story arc; they simply exist to service characters and add some humor to the episode.

So, yes, the script has eight story lines! (You may find more.) The structure could be diagrammed as A/A/B/B/B/C/C/C. Not the kind of story you're likely to see on Nickelodeon. But these types of complex structures are becoming more the norm in high-end half-hour comedies (especially on film shows that use very short scenes and lots of sets).

Story Elements

The episode uses a two-act structure.

In the Catherine A-story, the **inciting incident** is when Selina tells her staff she is going to adopt a dog to help her bond with her daughter. This information comes out as exposition with Amy in the first scene. This story seems to be about adopting a pet, but it is really about Selina's distant relationship with Catherine (and all of her human relationships). It's a metaphor for the soullessness of Washington power.

In the task force A-story, the **inciting incident** is when Jonah tells Selina that the president wants to know when she'll be announcing the new appointment to her clean jobs task force. This puts pressure on Selina to get the key approvals she'll need to ensure that the appointment doesn't create a political backlash for her.

Though Selina is driving almost every story in the episode, the writers use the various plot lines to service the other characters. Mike is tasked with announcing the appointment of Chuck Furnam as "the oil guy" on the task force. Amy must kill the "Hurricane Selina" name, and she also serves as Selina's confidant in the Catherine story. Jonah escalates Selina's rumored rift with the First Lady, and then escalates that story again in the second act when he tells everyone that the First Lady is also planning to adopt a dog. And Dan saves the day with a Machiavellian solution to the task force problem. Each story has a series of first act escalations.

In the task force story:

- a key senator rejects the idea of nominating Chuck Furnam.
- another senator rejects the idea of nominating Chuck Furnam.

- an oil lobbyist rejects the idea of nominating Chuck Furnam.
- Chuck Furnam leaks the news of his nomination.

As an aside, notice that Furnam "leaks" the news in a men's room, where men go to take a leak. That's never explicitly said in the script, but it's a subtle gag that I thought was worth pointing out. Nothing happens by accident in a well-written script.

In the Catherine story:

- Selina decides to use the dog adoption for publicity purposes (nothing she does is genuine)
- Selina's daughter arrives to have lunch with her mom, but is kept waiting
- Sue let's it slip that Selina is getting them a dog
- Selina has to cancel the mother-daughter lunch that was supposed to prove "there is nothing more important than Catherine" because "something more important than Catherine has just come up."

The first act also contains a **block comedy scene** at the dedication of a recreation center, where we learn that the senator it was named after was a pathological womanizer, and where everyone uses his widow as a prop. Dan coins it the "widow walk."

That gag is called back later when Selina uses Catherine for a widow walk. And in a way, her daughter is a metaphorical orphan [or widow] because of her dead relationship with her mom. This is the **subtext** of the script.

The **act break** is when Selina has to cancel lunch with her daughter to deal with the task force problem.

The second act introduces more twists and escalations in each A-story:

- Selina keeps pawning Catherine off on other people
- Catherine picks a dog that Amy and Selina hate
- Selina talks to Amy about Catherine instead of spending time with Catherine
- Dan suggests holding a dog naming contest to buy time on the Furnam announcement
- the senator pressures Selina to dump Chuck Furnam
- Catherine gets more frustrated as she watches Selina work the party crowd
- the White House wants the oil lobbyist for the task force position
- Dan uses guile to get the oil lobbyist to accept a non-official role, then uses him to change the senator's mind on Chuck Furnam
- In their moment together, Selina and Catherine have nothing to talk about
- Catherine learns that Selina is changing the name of a hurricane to protect her p.r. image
- Catherine confronts Selina

...all culminating in the 20-year anniversary party scene, where all the A and B-stories intersect and come to a head.

Another **subtext** of the script: whereas most people celebrate wedding anniversaries, Selina is married to her job – and that anniversary is the only important one in her life. This kind of subtext is lost on many viewers, but it makes the writing much richer for discerning fans.

The **climax** of the dog story is when Selina learns that the First Lady is also getting a dog, so Selina has to get rid of the rescue dog she just adopted, which upsets her daughter.

The **climax** of the task force story is when Dan tricks Senator Doyle into requesting that Selina put Chuck Furnam back on the task force.

The **resolution** of the two stories is that Selina scores a career success but at the expense of her relationship with her daughter. The B-stories also resolve, with Selina insisting that Mike adopt the rescue dog Catherine picked. Amy squelching the hurricane name, and the anniversary party being a non-diva success because the guests "definitely aren't having too much fun."

(Again, in another subtle metaphor, Selina gets rid of one rescue dog while rescuing another dog: the troubled Chuck Furnam appointment.)

Okay, so that's the mechanics of the story. But what is the episode really "about?"

I think it's more about Selina's empty relationship with her daughter and less about her career-based task force crisis. I say this for two reasons:

1. Selina will have many career crises like the task force, but she only has one child.
2. the writers tell us which story the episode is truly about in the title: "*Catherine.*"

ASSIGNMENT

CONTINUE WORKING ON YOUR OUTLINE, ADDING DESCRIPTION, JOKES, OR DIALOGUE LINES TO SCENES AS YOU THINK OF THEM. WHEN YOU HAVE A DRAFT OF YOUR OUTLINE, YOU SHOULD PUT IT AWAY FOR AT LEAST A DAY OR TWO TO CLEAR YOUR HEAD AND GET SOME PERSPECTIVE. YOU'RE PROBABLY CHOMPING AT THE BIT TO START YOUR FIRST DRAFT.

BUT NO, YOU'RE NOT THERE YET. THIS IS ONLY THE FIRST, ROUGH DRAFT OF YOUR OUTLINE. WHAT SOME WRITERS CALL A DUMP DRAFT (OR WORSE, A VOMIT DRAFT. YUCK!), WHERE EVERY THOUGHT YOU HAVE MADE IT INTO THE STARTING LINEUP. WE STILL HAVE SOME WORK TO DO BEFORE YOU'RE READY TO GO TO SCRIPT.

BE PATIENT. THE GRUNT WORK YOU PUT IN NOW WILL SAVE YOU LOTS OF HEADACHES AND SORROW LATER.

9

LAYERING YOUR STORY

INGREDIENTS:
-INTERNAL CONFLICT
-EMOTIONAL ARCS
-SUBTEXT
-METAPHORS
-SYMBOLISM

There's a scene in *Modern Family* when Cam and Mitchell have a flat tire and begin to change it themselves, and Cam uses that moment on bended-knee to propose to Mitchell. Maybe you saw it and thought, what a sweet moment. That's not just a sweet moment, it's a television work of art. That scene has comedy, irony, visual motifs, symbolism, metaphor, subtext, and a whole bunch of other cool writing devices that didn't just happen on the set. A writer, a writing staff, and a multi-talented crew all worked together to make this one shot magical.

I'll come back to this shot and explain why it's magical later. For now, let's get into our outline's polish pass.

Checking the Emotional Arcs

A lot of beginners write sitcom stories that they think are funny and forget that each story has to contain some nugget of believable dramatic conflict to carry the weight of an episode.

At their heart, all stories are about emotions: what your kids did that was cute and endearing, what that selfish jerk did to you in traffic that almost got you killed, what your boss did that was so upsetting it made you want to quit, what your boyfriend/girlfriend/spouse did that made you so jealous it almost broke up your relationship. The best stories – and hence the best sitcom episodes – are about an emotion that almost everyone can identify with and has a point of view or twist that makes it distinct enough to be worth sitting through for 22 minutes.

Go through your outline and make sure the A-story has a real, true-to-life and believable emotional arc. Make sure that the character grappling with these emotions is a major character in the series. Make sure that he/she takes some concrete action to fix the problem, even if that action initially makes things worse.

Then make sure there is a satisfying resolution to that character's arc. Again, not necessarily a happy/sappy ending (though sometimes those work well). But rather, an ending that the reader will not see coming yet will be happy it did.

The movie *Chinatown* has a satisfying ending even though it ends with the good guy (Evelyn Mulwray) getting murdered and the bad guy getting away with it. It was satisfying because it was sad, yet felt true and made a unique point about justice and corruption. Your outline isn't *Chinatown*, but it should have an ending that people will talk about, and feel was worthy of the journey.

Do a Conflict Tune-up

Now that you've looked for the big mistakes, take another

read through your outline to look for the more nuanced – but just as fatal – mistakes that writers sometimes make.

The first thing to ask yourself is: does my story contain a compelling *external* conflict? By conflict I don't mean a lot of people bickering with each other. Conflict means that a character has a very clear want or goal, and a very clear obstacle in her way that keeps her from achieving it. In *Veep*, Selina's goal is often to get some task force or new policy launched to further her political ambition. The obstacle is usually some D.C. power player who has a different goal or political agenda. Their goals are in conflict, so they are too.

In *The Big Bang Theory*, the conflict can be as simple as Amy wanting to move her relationship with Sheldon to another level. In *Parks and Recreation,* it's often Leslie trying to advance some government initiative that's important to her without getting too much push-back from her coworkers or the citizens of Pawnee.

Whatever your conflict is, make sure it has vital meaning to the character, and make sure the obstacle in her way is big enough to keep her from achieving that goal for 22 minutes or more. *This is another key concept.* What often sinks a spec script is that the conflict isn't strong enough, which means that by the second act there aren't enough believable obstacles to throw in the character's way, and the writer has to start inventing trite, artificial ones.

Example:

Leslie Knope (*Parks and Recreation*) wants to convince Pawnee's high school students that government is an honorable and rewarding career choice. Okay, that clearly sounds like something Leslie would think and do. But what is the obstacle in her way? The students don't agree that government work is a viable career. She makes a classroom presentation, and they are bored by it? This was an actual A-story in one student's outline, and as I expected, by the time he got to the middle of the outline, the story ran out of steam. So, he had to invent unbelievable escalations to fill scenes. I'm not picking on him – he had good B-stories and came up with some funny ideas. But the A-story wasn't strong enough to support an episode and the plot cratered.

So just because you have a 6-page, spell checked outline containing eighteen scenes and some pretty good gags, doesn't mean you have a working storyline. Make sure your conflict is compelling and the obstacles in your character's path are big enough to give you really interesting escalations and twists. Those are just as important as your premise – if not more so.

Internal Conflict vs. External Conflict

The other key component to your conflict is who the character is in conflict with.

Emotional conflict is an storyline that plays out inside a character's brain. Hence, the term *internal conflict*. It's different than *external conflict*, where you are at odds with another person, group, or environment. But sometimes a writer tries to put their character in conflict with themself.

That can be done, but boy it's tricky!

So, I suggest that you embody their antagonist in one person or one very defined entity (a government office, a company, a school clique, etc.). In other words, an *external conflict*. Make sure that entity is personified in at least one person. And make sure the antagonist is an equal or greater match for your protagonist.

Often, due to story escalations, the person (or entity) that your protagonist was in conflict with at first, morphs into someone else or a larger group of people. It's important to be clear on this when it happens. Your conflict cannot be sharp and crisp if you don't know who it is with.

Last, make sure you know how the conflict resolves, and what the outcome is. You may think this is obvious, but you'd be surprised how often I read an outline that sort of peters out with no real conclusion. It's as if the writer got eight scenes into the last act and thought, *It feels like I must be near the end by now, so I better wrap things up.*

That's the way to end a meal or a jog, but not a story.

Exercise: Fill out the Conflict Tune-up Worksheet posted in the Resources section to see how clear your conflicts are. If you can fill in something for each blank space and it makes sense to you, you probably have a workable conflict in each story.

Try to use as many *external* conflicts as possible. People in conflict with other people almost always plays better on screen than a character wrestling with their own conscience, insecurity, or anger. Even a drunk stumbling around alone at home is in conflict with something else: liquor.

When Jackson Mason of *A Star Is Born* commits suicide, yes, he's in conflict with his internal demons. But he's also in conflict with his wife Ally's career and her manager, Rez, who thinks Jack is holding her back. That is external conflict.

Here's a sample *Conflict Tune-up* I created for *30 Rock*:

A-STORY

THIS STORY'S LEAD CHARACTER IS JACK DONAGHY

HIS GOAL IS TO INCREASE NBC'S 'URBAN DEMO-
GRAPHIC' BY GETTING TO KNOW HOW BLACK PEOPLE
THINK

HE IS IN CONFLICT WITH THE BLACK PEOPLE HE
MEETS AT A HARLEM BASKETBALL GAME BECAUSE
JACK IS A WHITE CORPORATE ELITIST

TWO OBSTACLES ARE 1) JACK'S WHITE CEO
MENTALITY 2) HE KNOWS LITTLE ABOUT BASKETBALL

BY MID-STORY, HE IS IN CONFLICT WITH HIMSELF
BECAUSE HE WANTS SPIKE LEE TO LIKE HIM
      BY LATE STORY, HE IS IN CONFLICT WITH THE
REFEREE AT A KNICK GAME SPIKE TAKES HIM TO
BECAUSE THIS PERSON THINKS JACK TRIPPED HIM ON
PURPOSE
      LATER, HE IS IN CONFLICT WITH SPIKE LEE
      BECAUSE JACK GOT HIM EJECTED FROM MADISON
SQ GARDEN FOREVER AND SPIKE ENDS THEIR BROMANCE,
HURTING JACK'S FEELINGS
      THE CONFLICT RESOLVES WHEN JACK REPLACES
SPIKE WITH JIMMY FALLON

For your homework, I want you to look at your outline with a
fresh set of eyes and the wisdom of knowing your series even
better than you did when you started outlining your episode.

Believe me, the grunt work you do now will pay off handsomely when you're writing scripted scenes in Act Two and you
don't have to then go back to the drawing board to fix a problematic beat or storyline.

Magic Moments

Now, let's go back to that moment of Cam proposing to
Mitchell. If you saw the episode, the setup was that once
marriage became legal in California, the two men who'd been
living together for ages, were more than ready to move to the
next step in their relationship.

But who was going to propose to who? In a two-gender relationship, most often it's the man proposing to the woman.
However, in a same sex relationship, someone has to take the
initiative.

So, this storyline found the two men each conspiring with

family members to surprise the other with a ring. And almost everyone else in the family knew it but them.

On the night that they both secretly planned to take the big plunge, their car gets a flat tire. Stuck on a dark, out of the way road, they set out to change it themselves. Then, suddenly, they find themselves kneeling in front of the flat tire face to face, and they both realize it's time to propose to each other.

Modern Family *(20th Century Fox Television)*

But what makes it so magical in my opinion is the visual imagery going on in the shot. Let's take a look at that photo again.

What's the first thing you notice about this unusual proposal, other than that both parties are kneeling? There's no ring. But if you look closer, you'll see that there is. The tire. Not just the round shape of the tire but look at the white wall and the metal rim. Conventional tires have one thick white wall ring. But the design and lighting on this tire makes it appear to have TWO RINGS...

If you think that was just a happy accident, my guess is, it wasn't. It's framed too perfectly. Someone had to conceive of that shot and then get the set designers to bring it to life, the camera crew to capture it with the proper lighting, and a talented director to block and shoot it so the rings are in frame. It's never mentioned in dialogue, and I'd venture to guess that 90% of the people who saw that episode never knew it was there. But they saw it subliminally. And for those of us who did catch it, it adds symbolism and subtext to an otherwise pedestrian marriage proposal.

All that captured in one shot of one beat. That's the type of storytelling I love to watch. And while I can't say it for certain, I'd be willing to bet that the idea started with the episode's writer.

ASSIGNMENT

WATCH – 2 EPISODES OF YOUR SERIES AND COMPARE THEM TO YOUR OUTLINE FOR STYLE AND PACE.

WRITE – GO THROUGH YOUR OUTLINE AND MAKE SURE THERE IS A TRUE-TO-LIFE AND BELIEVABLE EMOTIONAL ARC FOR EACH A AND B PLOT.

WRITE – FILL OUT THE *CONFLICT TUNE-UP WORKSHEET* IN THE RESOURCES SECTION OR DOWNLOAD A COPY OF THE *WORKSHEET* FOUND AT WWW.KEVINKELTON.COM/LINKS

10

POLISHING THE OUTLINE

INGREDIENTS:
—TIME
—PATIENCE
—ATTENTION TO DETAIL

Policing Your Stories

Once you've fine-tuned your conflict and made sure your escalations are good enough to keep things going for two or three acts, it's time to "police" your stories to make sure each plotline has all the elements of a good story.

Here is a list of policing questions to ask yourself. For each question, make sure you are satisfied with the answer:

- *Does your story have a clear inciting incident?* It need not happen on screen, but it must be referenced in the body of your script.
- *What is your story about? Does it communicate a clear theme? Is it believable?*

- *Does your story rely on trite TV tropes, or is it original?*
- *Are there beats of each story in every act?*
- *Does each scene logically lead to the next?* A good story is like a line of dominos falling; each scene of an individual storyline has to cause the next to happen.
- *Do you utilize every major character in at least one storyline?*
- *Is there an emotional arc for at least one character in every A and B-story?*
- *Does the chronology of the story make sense? Do your "day" and "night" scenes coordinate into a natural timeline?* I've seen movies in which there seems to be 3 days in the plot but 4-6 nights! This sometimes is caused by editing in post. But as the writer you want to make sure your stories live in real time and space.
- *Do characters speak to themselves?* This one is a big sore point for me. People rarely speak to themselves, and certainly not about anything important. If your character is advancing the plot by "thinking out loud," you as a writer need to think again. Figure out a way to get someone in the room with them. Knowing how to create and use confidantes is a critical skill in scene writing.
- *Does your plot rely too much on coincidences?* If so, try to extract every coincidence that works in favor of the lead character. An audience will buy a coincidence that impedes the character from achieving their goal, but they will disbelieve and resent coincidences that magically help the character.
- *Will the resolution be satisfying to the viewer?* That doesn't mean a "happy ending." It means an ending that has power and meaning is worthy of the time the viewer spent to get there.

If you really want to put your story to the test, have someone else read it and then answer those questions for you. Or have them read your answers and see if they agree.

Entrances and Exits

It's ease to lose track of entrances and exits while you are writing an outline when you're focused on tracking the story, not on being a character traffic cop.

But when you get around to writing the script, things will go smoother if you already know who is in each scene and how/why they got there. I often see *Modern Family* outlines where Claire goes over to Gloria's house for little or no reason, just so they can have a scene together. But even in the closest families, real world daughters don't just show up at their mother-in-law's house for no apparent reason. And just saying she came by to drop off a cake isn't enough; you have to think out the real motivation of why people are changing their natural locations to be in a scene.

In *Seinfeld,* it was okay for Kramer to barge through Jerry's door for a flimsy reason – that was part of the bizarre reality of that series and the essence of his character. But you rarely saw George or Elaine just show up without some logical reason – to go to a movie or party with Jerry, to ask an important favor, to complain about something big that just happened to them, etc. Of course, in the real-world family and friends more often call or text about such things. But in a dramatic work, it's best to put your characters in the same room. Phone calls and texting should only be used when absolutely necessary for the plot.

Even if they were doing something mundane like Elaine coming to Jerry's place after work or George coming to complain about a girl, you felt it was believable in the context of their day-to-day relationships. But another series may not share that casual show-up-whenever reality. So, if a Tom Haverford has since left the *Parks and Recreation* department for another job, you can't just have him hanging out at the office without a believable and interesting reason. I mean, *you can*, but professional readers will spot it and grade you down for it. I know I would.

Or, using *Modern Family* as an example again, when less-experienced writers want to get several family members into the same room for a scene they need to advance their plot, they write in a "family dinner" scene. I suppose that makes sense, but it's a very weak and non-creative way to do it. Unless there's an inventive and compelling reason for Jay to have his two children and their families over for dinner, I'm reading the scene and thinking "lazy writing."

Beyond the test of logic, there's the equally important test of "is it creative and interesting?" When George and Elaine showed up to go with Jerry to a movie, the writers always mentioned the movie title (usually a funny one) and had them say something about the movie that made the moment funny. There's no bigger sin in comedy writing than to let a great comedic opportunity go to waste.

Here's another set of policing questions to ask yourself about your lead character's arc:

- Is the story problem based on the protagonist's (generally your series lead) primary flaw?
- Does the protagonist drive the story? Is that clear in all the scenes?
- Is it clear up front what the protagonist wants?
- Is it clear what's at stake (respect, job, sex)? In other words, is there an emotional component?
- Does the conflict arise because the protagonist hoisted themself with their own petard? In other words, did his/her major flaw get them into this mess?
- Do things escalate in the middle? Is each complication worse than the one before, requiring greater effort on the part of the protagonist to overcome?

Once you are satisfied with the answers to all these questions, you'll be ready to proceed to starting your script.

If you are not satisfied with one or more answers, you have some work to do. Here are some helpful tricks.

Casting Your Script

If you haven't done it already, cast your original characters (the ones you've made up for this episode) in your head with real actors. Do not (I can't stress this enough) put casting suggestions in your script—unless it's a specific stunt casting choice, like Leslie Knope visiting D.C. and meeting then V.P. Joe Biden, or Liz Lemon running into NBC news anchor (at the time) Brian Williams in the halls of 30 Rock.

By the way, if you DO stunt cast your spec – a dicey proposition – try to choose characters that we can reasonably believe the series can get. So, you can put in a scene with *Young Sheldon's* boy genius Sheldon Cooper meeting Dr. Fauci for a moment; I'd make that leap that they could get him. But don't have him get babysat by Scarlett Johansson or Halle Berry. They most likely wouldn't do that show. If the reader has to stop and wonder, *Hmm...would that person really do a guest spot on this series?* You've taken the reader out of the moment and probably diminished your writing in their eyes.

Now, back to *non-stunt casting,* casting. Once you've come up with an idea for that maître 'd or school psychologist character that we'll meet briefly in your second act, come up with the perfect actor to play him/her. Think about how they'd talk and dress in the role. Write the character as if that actor were going to play the part. So yeah, make the hunky diving instructor of *Emily in Paris'* Emily Cooper a version of Timotheé Chalamet in your mind. You can even envision the character as a version of Chalamet's character from *The French Dispatch* if it will help you nail the voice and attitude. Don't get me wrong and think I'm telling you to plagiarize characters – I'm not. *Because the words you put in his mouth and the actions he takes in his scenes will be your original creation.* But the voice will be more clearly defined in your mind as you write them, and hence in the reader's mind when they're reading the script.

And in case you didn't know, TV and film writers do this all the time. I call it "casting on spec" and it's a perfectly valid way to create original characters, whether you use an actress or one of the characters she's played. Eventually, as you write, the actor/character you are modeling the role after will dissipate into the recesses of your mind and the new character will emerge. But if you wrote it with Steve Carrell in mind and someone who reads it says, *"Wow, what a perfect role for Steve Carrell! I could really see him playing it."* You'll know you nailed his voice and wrote a script that jumps off the page.

The Character Test

Next you should look at the characters in your episode to make sure they're believable. Of course, the series' regular and semi-regular characters are already well-defined since the series has been on the air for several seasons.

But it never ceases to amaze me how spec writers will misunderstand who the characters are. This is a primary reason that spec scripts are tossed in the No Way pile.

The biggest offense is taking a somewhat dumb character and having him/her behave like a blathering moron. Don't do that! Whether it's Andy in *Parks and Recreation* or Schmidt in *New Girl*, make sure you haven't given this person lines and actions that are so stupid it makes them unbelievable in the context of that series' reality.

This is a difficult but important concept to grasp. Every TV series (and movie, novel, and play) has an artificial reality that approximates the real world but is slightly different. In the real world, people would fire Tom Haverford (*Parks and Recreation*), sue Michael Scott (*The Office*) for sexual harassment, and slap Sheldon Cooper (*The Big Bang Theory*) on a regular basis.

But in a TV series, there is a false reality that allows characters to do things we can't get away with in the real world. *That doesn't mean the entire world of the series is unbelievable.* That world bends certain social conventions for entertainment purposes but stays true to most social rules and accepted behaviors so that we can identify with the story. Even a surreal show like *Sponge Bob* has to follow certain accepted societal norms so we understand that if Squidward is too mean to a Crusty Crab customer, he could get fired. Otherwise, there are no social rules, and no one would care what the characters do.

Yet even in the fictionalized reality of a comedy series, characters have to behave in a way that makes sense in that world.

Let me give another example: I had a student write a *Modern Family* spec where Manny and Luke were running against each other for class president. Okay, that is believable. But when Luke cheated, my student wrote a scene where Gloria was so upset, she urged Manny to get revenge with a Columbian-style political assassination. Now of course the writer had Gloria saying it somewhat tongue-in-cheek; Gloria didn't intend to have Manny act on the suggestion. But just having Gloria say something like that is, for me, far outside of even her fiery temperament. It wasn't believable to me, even in the context of a TV sitcom. So, we urged the writer to cut the line.

In doing so, she also took a broader look at how Gloria and Claire were overreacting to their sons running against each other in a middle-school election, and she found more believable emotional arcs for them. In the rough draft they were possessed backstage moms, doing things no thinking mother in the real world would ever do. But by the next draft they were behaving more like real moms would in that situation. Still a bit overly involved in the election, still funny, but a lot more believable.

Sometimes just removing or adjusting a false beat can make all the difference in a story.

If you wrote a *Parks and Recreation* that has Andy saying or doing something dumber than anything Forest Gump ever said or did, you should rethink it. Andy is slightly dim but not mentally challenged. If your *Modern Family* has Cam behaving like a (excuse the crude term) flaming queen, you are misunderstanding who he is. If it has Claire yelling at Phil and insulting his masculinity, again, you are probably missing the true essence of her character and their relationship. If Manny is saying things way too mature for any young teenage boy, you are writing a sitcomy version of him that really isn't true to the series.

So read through your outline and make sure your characters are true to the series. If you have any doubt about a character's behavior or a joke, ask us (on Blackboard). Because if you leave these types of tonal mistakes in your outline, they will only get magnified once you begin writing the script.

Avoid Tropes

Hopefully, you've heard of TV tropes. A *trope* is a common theme or device used in storytelling, such as the bumbling husband/dad, the prudish librarian, the hooker with a heart of gold, or the gruff police captain. Because there are so darn many of them, it's sometimes impossible to avoid every single trope that exists. But at least *try*. Too many tropes will make your writing seem formulaic and familiar. Professional readers will spot them in a second and take points off if you pepper your script with them.

Theme, Subtext & Symbolism

Of course, every series has an overarching theme that infuses that series with meaning. If you read interviews by the people

THE SITCOM WRITER'S COOKBOOK

who've created great shows, you'll always find that they had a very specific theme in mind when they wrote the pilot and pitched the series to the network. Each episode should either reinforce that theme, or communicate a new theme that ties into the overall theme of the series.

While some people think sitcom episodes don't need grand themes or the subtlety of subtext, having them definitely makes your writing sample stronger. If you watch the best shows – the ones that consistently win Emmys and Golden Globes – you'll find that their scripts are more than just a collection of funny scenes and one-liners. They say something about the human condition. (Even if it's a highly cynical view of the human condition, as a *Curb Your Enthusiasm* or *Veep* script might show.) And they do it in a clever, subtle way.

There are two types of themes: expressed (in dialog) and implied (not said).

So, I want you to mine your story for its theme and express that in a clear sentence. Examples might be:

"LOVE MEANS NEVER HAVING TO SAY YOU'RE SORRY." (AN *EXPRESSED* THEME)

"BEING A FAMILY IS ABOUT SHARING LOVE AND ACCEPTANCE, NOT JUST SHARING THE SAME DNA." (AN *IMPLIED* THEME)

"HAVING A BOYFRIEND/GIRLFRIEND DOESN'T MAKE YOU WHOLE."

Whatever yours is, I want you to write it in a short, clear sentence and stick it to your computer screen. Yes, literally scotch tape it or Post-it Note it right to your screen. Then, I want you to go through each scene of your A-story and try to find some element of that theme in it. If it's not there, add something to the scene to help bring that theme to life. It needn't be expressed in a line of dialog, either – it can be an action, a reaction, an attitude, or something else that "lives between the lines."

Here's a classic example: *In the 1960s, a middle-aged married couple is on an elevator. The man is wearing a hat. They are riding in silence. On the 8th floor, a woman gets on the elevator, and the man takes off his hat.*

That one action tells you a lot about the couple's relationship and speaks to the greater theme of marriage and taking your spouse for granted.

While you're not going to find something that vivid for every scene, try to find a few places in your story where you can anchor the theme in some action, attitude, or symbolic visual. Even if you're writing a *Bob's Burgers* or *South Park*, industry readers will spot that and be impressed by it. And you'll be proud of it.

A great example of subtext and symbolism in a half-hour episode is the *Modern Family* episode, "The Old Wagon." Watch it and look for the symbolism of Luke's jar of sunshine, Phil's time machine, and the subtext of Gloria's chocolate milk with salt – all wrapped in a theme about the difficulty of letting go of the things and people you love.

Adding Laughs

Okay, by now you are sick of talking about your outline. You want to get to writing the script, and I don't blame you.

So, we're going to start writing the script *in the outline*. How? By going through and adding lines of dialogue or funny business to each scene.

Let's be clear, when you developed your outline, I limited you to six pages. The reason is that too long an outline makes it difficult to follow the story - both for the reader and you.

As you know from the examples you've seen, professional outlines can run 8 to 12 to even 16 pages, though a 16-page outline is very excessive for a 34-page script.

But now I'm going to let you push your outlines beyond six pages to add in details that will end up in your script. So, go back through it and turn all those *Mitch says* descriptions into a snappy line of dialog, so that...

MITCH SAYS THAT CAM IS BEING OVERLY PROTECTIVE OF LILY.

becomes...

MITCH: "THE GIRL IS SIX. SHE DOESN'T NEED A FORCE FIELD AROUND HER. ESPECIALLY ONE THAT WEARS DAD JEANS."

Don't do it for every "says" line in your outline but do try to add good jokes where you can. Once you are writing your script, you will grab for those pre-written lines like lifesavers in an ocean.

Also look for places where you can add "business" to the scene. If you don't recognize the term, "business" is those funny little actions or bits that characters do while they are talking. It can be as simple as trying to swat a fly, to something as complicated as having a character do a pre-jog hamstring stretch by putting their foot on a supermarket checkout conveyor belt that suddenly begins to move.

While half-hour shows tend to be very verbal forms of comedy, good visual bits can make a scene and an episode. But when we develop our outlines, we often get caught up in the who-says-what aspect of storytelling and forget that people need to move around and do interesting things in our scenes.

So go through and see where you can add an interesting bit of business or a visual gag.

ASSIGNMENT

POLICE YOUR OUTLINE BY APPLYING THE LISTS OF QUESTIONS TO YOUR STORIES AND FIX WHAT NEEDS TO BE FIXED. DETERMINE THE THEME OF YOUR A-STORY AND WRITE A DECLARATIVE SENTENCE EXPRESSING IT. THEN GO THROUGH

YOUR OUTLINE AND TRY TO PLANT SUBTEXT AND SYMBOLISM THAT HELP EXPRESS THAT THEME THROUGHOUT THE SCRIPT.

WRITE — PUNCH-UP YOUR OUTLINE ONCE AGAIN, TRYING TO ADD TWO OR MORE LAUGHS TO EVERY SCENE. YOUR OUTLINE WILL NOW BE LONGER THAN SIX PAGES, AND THAT'S OKAY. YOU PUT IN THE WORK TO MAKE THE FOUNDATION OF YOUR STORY TREE SOLID. NOW YOU CAN HANG SOME TINSEL ON THE BRANCHES.

THE FIRST DRAFT

The Main Course

THE FIRST DRAFT

11

MORPHING YOUR SCRIPT

The Kelton Method

So, you've got your polished outline, and you're happy with it. How do you proceed? Simple: keep doing what you've been doing but in script format.

The Kelton Method

What I absolutely don't want you to do is start a new document. Blank pages are the number one cause of writers' block. So, I've created a system to do away with them.

Instead, I developed a system over the years to avoid ever having to look at a blank screen once I have started a beat sheet. I just never leave the beat sheet. The beat sheet morphs into the outline, and the outline morphs into the script. I call it *The Kelton Method*.

This trick may seem simple – even simplistic – until you try it. The beauty of it is you can always see where you're going right in front of you – there is always a destination on the horizon...in words...all the way to the end.

In fact, if you think it may help you, go to the end of your outline *right now* and type the words:

END OF SHOW

Go on, do it. It's okay, the sitcom police will not arrest you. Now you have a target *in typed out words* to aim for.

I know you probably feel silly doing this – just like you felt silly and self-conscious doing your first "I'm a tree" exercise in acting class or doing the Macarena at Club Med. But once you actually get up and do it, you find it's not as dumb as you think. You actually start to lose your inhibitions and get into it. (I speak from experience on that Macarena thing.)

Expanding Each Scene

The next step is to take a scene – any scene – and start turning the bits of dialogue you already have written in paragraph form into formatted dialogue.

So, this...

> STUDIO BACK STAGE - MOMENTS LATER
>
> LIZ SPOTS DOTCOM AND TRACY MOVING TRACY'S LUGGAGE AND BELONGINGS INTO HIS DRESSING ROOM. TRACY TELLS KENNETH HE'S GOING TO BE USING THE BACKSTAGE KITCHEN AREA AS HIS NEW BATHROOM, "SO SPREAD THE WORD." LIZ ASKS WHAT'S GOING ON AND LEARNS THAT TRACY'S WIFE KICKED HIM OUT FOR "MINISTERING" TO A TRANSVESTITE PROSTITUTE. DOTCOM: "HE DOESN'T MESS WITH THEM - HE JUST TRIES TO GET THEM INTO COMPUTER SCHOOL." BUT IT TURNS OUT THAT A PAPARAZZI SNAPPED A PHOTO OF TRACY WITH THE PROSTI-TUTE AND ANGIE SAW IT IN THE TABLOIDS, SO NOW HE'S A MAN WITHOUT A HOME.

starts to become this...

INT. STUDIO BACK STAGE - MOMENTS LATER

Liz sees Kenneth, Dotcom and Tracy moving Tracy's luggage and belongings into his dressing room.

TRACY

Yo Ken, I'm gonna need to use this kitchen area as my bathroom. Spread the word.

Liz asks what's going on and learns that Tracy's wife kicked him out for "ministering" to a transvestite prostitute.

DOTCOM

He doesn't mess with them - he just tries to get them into computer school.

But it turns out that a paparazzi snapped a photo of Tracy with the prostitute and Angie saw it in the tabloids, so now he's a man without a home.

As you can see, it's still missing some dialogue. That's because I'm (you're) still writing it. But by writing it directly in the outline shell, you're never starting a scene from scratch. You're just adding dialogue and jokes to what you already have.

As you write, you may move things around, invent new beats or jokes, think of a better way to do something. That's fine. The outline is not carved in stone. It's just a road map. If you spot a better path to go along the way, go there see where it leads. As long as it doesn't take you too far off course, go with it. If you get stuck in a scene, move to another one. There's no law that says you have to write in chronological order.

If you invent something new and cool in the second act that should have been set up earlier, go back and set it up now. Boom –

you just wrote a call-back! Some of my best call-backs weren't really call-backs at all – they were jokes I invented while writing the second act that I then went back and laid into an earlier scene. Again, no law that says you can't write the punchline before the set-up. (Comedy writers do that all the time.)

Pretty soon, your long paragraph blocks will become leaner as you turn outline dialogue into script dialogue and add more.

You'll keep doing this until every beat has been morphed into dialogue and staged bits. By that time, you should have three acts (or a Cold Opening and two acts) and about 32-35 pages. Congratulations – you just finished a first draft. (Or, as I prefer, "rough draft.")

Will it be perfect? Of course not. Hence the label "rough." But you'll have laid out the basics of your story in script format, found a lot of good dialogue along the way, and it will look like something familiar to you, because you've already read (or by now should have read) several production scripts from the series.

If you try this basic system, you should find that writing the script is not nearly as daunting as it may feel at first. You don't have to write thirty-two new pages. You just take the eight or more outline pages and slowly build them out. And if you go long, no problem – that just means you'll have the added luxury of being able to cut plenty of junky stuff and still come in at 32-35.

Scriptwriting Software

There are several industry standard software programs for scriptwriting, the most popular being **Final Draft** and **Movie Magic**. One of the great features of Final Draft is that it actually has some preset formats for a few major network series, and they add new ones with every version update. The downside of these programs is that they are costly.

You may be able to find a free download of a basic script writing program online. If you are just dipping your toes into TV writing and don't mind a little extra hassle, you can probably find a free MS Word template. Here's an **article** on how to set up Word for screenplay format. I've never tried this, but it might just work.

But whatever writing software you use, even if it's Word or Pages, please don't submit material that doesn't conform exactly to your show's script format. It may sound nit-picky, but it's really distracting to read a script that looks like this:

SHELDON: WITTY SHELDON DIALOGUE HERE.
AMY: EQUALLY WITTY AMY DIALOGUE GOES HERE. AND MORE HERE. AND MORE ALL THE WAY OVER HERE.

Or this:

SHELDON
WITTY SHELDON DIALOGUE HERE.
AMY
EQUALLY WITTY AMY DIALOGUE GOES HERE. AND MORE HERE. AND MORE ALL THE WAY OVER HERE.

Or this:

SHELDON
WITTY SHELDON DIALOGUE HERE.
AMY
EQUALLY WITTY AMY DIALOGUE GOES HERE.

Character names and dialogue are never centered. So don't submit anything that resembles that. Dress your script for success.

If you have questions about script formatting that you can't find answers for in your own show's production scripts, check out

How *Not* to Write a Screenplay by Denny Martin Flinn. (A great resource to have on your bookshelf.)

ASSIGNMENT

WRITE — GO THROUGH YOUR OUTLINE AND TURN ALL OF YOUR SNIPPETS OF DIALOGUE AND NEW JOKES INTO SCRIPT FORMAT. (SEE EXAMPLE ABOVE.) THAT SHOULD MAKE YOUR OUTLINE SHELL BEGIN TO LOOK LIKE SOMETHING RESEMBLING A SCRIP AND SHOULD NOW BE AROUND FIFTEEN PAGES — ALMOST HALF OF A COMPLETED SCRIPT! (AND I BET IT WILL FEEL GOOD TO LOOK AT.)

WRITE — YOUR COLD OPENING (OR THE FIRST SCENE OF YOUR EPISODE) COMPLETELY IN SCRIPT FORMAT. THIS IS DONE RIGHT INSIDE THE POLISHED OUTLINE DOC. NO NEW DOC NECESSARY.

12

WRITING GREAT CHARACTERS

Okay, so you've finally started writing scenes and dialog in script format, and it feels good. Maybe you are loving the lines and jokes you are coming up with, or maybe you are struggling a bit. Either is okay at this point – it's only a first draft, and what counts most now is story, story, story.

But you may be writing for these characters for the first time and still trying to capture their voice. How do you do that?

Read, Dammit, Read!

The best – really the only way – to capture and duplicate the voice of a TV character is to read produced episodes. Sure, it helps to watch the series and get the voice in your head. But you won't know what that voice *looks like on paper* unless you inundate yourself with show scripts. There is a visual style to a character's speech patterns that is almost impossible to duplicate unless you *see their voice,* as well as hear it.

I used to visualize dialogue in my mind as I watched a TV show or movie. I don't do that anymore (the habit was driving me crazy after a while), but it served me well in learning what great dialogue looks like. I strongly suggest you try it.

The other thing you'll learn is that *the way the character talks on paper* is much more dignified than what you hear on screen. This is an important concept to grasp. A comedy character can seem like a dimwitted buffoon until you see how their lines read. To understand a character, you need to see their lines in print.

Rocky is a great example of this. The movie can make Rocky Balboa seem like a low-IQ, punched out idiot. But when you read the script, there is a dignity and wisdom in the words that can be obscured by Stallone's performance. Don't get me wrong, I'm not criticizing his performance – it was excellent. I'm simply saying that you can miss the essence of a character if you only hear the words, see the body language, or how other characters look at them. But when you *see the dialogue* in script form, you get a new, and sometimes better, understanding of who the character is and how they communicate and think.

Defend Your Character's Dignity

Another great example of a misunderstood character is Cam on *Modern Family*. I read a lot of spec *Modern Family* outlines and scripts, and I'm constantly amazed at how writers misperceive this character and strip him of his dignity. Because Cam is gay and because Eric Stonehill plays him with an affected gay intonation, inexperienced writers often perceive him as (please excuse the pejorative) a flamer. But he isn't. Yes, he is a gay man and proud of it. Yes, he is the more domesticated "homemaker" of the couple. And yes, he has an artistic eye and nurturing parenting style. But he's a dignified man, not an over-the-top drag queen.

Yet in student written outline after outline, I see Cam being written that way. I see him being dressed up in outlandish outfits, being made to act overtly catty and prissy, and only relating to other people in terms of swishy gay stereotypes. I don't know why people perceive Cam as swishy (as opposed to Mitchell, whom people tend to see as a more 3-dimensional character). I never saw

Cam that way, even in episodes that touch on issues of sexuality. (The Season 4 "Yard Sale" episode where the adults are trying to determine the sexuality of Alex's new boyfriend comes to mind.) But I suspect it's because they are hearing Stonehill's voice and not listening to his words.

Case in point: one student wrote a *Modern Family* outline with a family Olympics storyline that had Cam planning an elaborate opening ceremonies with costumes and dance routines. I don't believe that the real series would do that. Sure, the show might do one or two opening ceremonies gags. But an entire C-story where Cam stages the whole production, oblivious to the fact that it's ridiculous to do that for a family sports competition? That doesn't seem like the *Modern Family* I see every week.

Another student chose to write a B-story about Cam and Mitch having a "date night" out, and guess where they went: a gay bar. Maybe it's me, but I just don't believe that's a choice that those two characters would ever make.

Now let's contrast that to how the show really depicts those characters. Yes, they are gay men, but not cartoonishly so. Case in point: the Season 5 opening episode, "Suddenly, Last Summer," where Cameron and Mitch were both secretly planning to propose to each other. Cam was going to do it at a restaurant; Mitch's plan was to pop the question after a home-cooked meal. But they ended up proposing to each other while changing a flat tire. The flat tire scene wasn't about them calling AAA or fumbling with the tools or fretting about getting dirty. No, they handled the flat tire the way most men would: they got out of the car and did it. (Finally coming face-to-face with each other on bended knee as they knelt down to change the tire.) In fact, that entire B-story could have been done with a heterosexual couple and been just as believable. It wasn't about being gay; it was about being in love.

If you read enough *Modern Family* scripts (or really pay attention to the character in the show), you'll see that Cam has a dignity and self-image that is much more than the one-dimensional character often found in spec scripts. He was a high school athlete, dated women at one time, and is a bright, witty, thoughtful, and competent man. Sure, he has a flair for theatrics. But when his theatrical side got the better of him during his day as a substitute history teacher, he dressed up as George Washington, not Dolly Madison.

I also see starting writers depict Claire Dunphy as more nasty and catty than she really is in the series, Gloria more crazed and insensitive, and Phil as much more of a henpecked buffoon than I perceive any of them to be. These storylines miss the core dignity of the characters.

The same is true with Andy in *Parks and Recreation*. While Andy is clearly not the brightest star in the sky, he's not a mentally challenged town idiot. Yet, like the others, I see student storylines riddled with Andy jokes that make him out to be something akin to Bull on *Night Court*.

Writing Day Players

Okay, so I hope all that makes sense in terms of writing for existing series characters. But what if your story involves creating a new character (or characters) for your episode?

Characters that are created for one episode are called *day players*. (Well, that's what the actor is called. But for our purposes I'll use that term for the character, too.) I've also heard them called "one-shots."

If you're developing a day-player character, even for just a scene or two, you still want them to come alive just as the regulars do.

Obviously, this is more challenging because the reader doesn't have an actor in mind when reading the day-player in the script. But no, do not – do NOT – cast your day-players with famous actors you think would be right for the role. (Unless you are clearly stunt casting your script, which is dicey in a spec but sometimes appropriate.)

Instead, you need to do your homework and create a great character on the page. But how?

The trick is not just to arrive at that scene and quickly stick in a stock day-player character who will conveniently (for you) service that moment in the story. You know the type of characters I mean: the pompously rude maitre 'd, the harried supermarket checker, the brusque school principal, the impatient hotel desk clerk. Because real people aren't just rude, or just harried, or just brusque, or just impatient. Real people are multidimensional, and the characters you create should be, too.

So instead of defining the character by their attitude in just that scene and that moment, think about who that character would be at the beginning of the episode (before they meet your series regular). Who they were the week before the episode began, and who they'll be after your series characters leave their lives forever. You don't need to write a 10-page bio – or even write a bio at all – but you do need to put some real thought into who these people would be *if they were a series regular*. What's their life POV? Who are they when they are *not* angry at Leslie Knope in a city council meeting or arguing with Claire Dunphy at the grocery store?

A good writing technique is to take that day-player character, who is going to clash with your series regular and write a scene with them and the series regular in a totally different situation that could have taken place days earlier. Then, see how they relate. This is not a scene for your script; it's simply an exercise to learn more about the character *before* you actually start writing them into your episode.

So as a writing exercise, put that maitre 'd in a DMV line with your series regular, where they are both in agreement about the long wait. Or put your grocery store checker on a first date with your series lead. Or put the school principal in the stands of a little league game with your series character where they both think the umpire is screwing up the game. See who these two people are when they are in agreement and hitting it off. That will make how you write their moment of conflict in your script more authentic and hopefully more interesting.

Is it extra work? Sure. But if you can create original characters in your spec script that jump off the page, it will lift your script in the eyes of producers and agents. Maybe they'll wonder how you'd handle writing a pilot or a movie script. Which means you're not just showcasing your episodic writing in your spec, you're showcasing yourself as a writer.

ASSIGNMENT

AFTER YOU'VE FINISHED WRITING THE COLD OPENING OR THE FIRST TWO SCENES OF YOUR SCRIPT, NOW *WRITE THE LAST SCENE AND TAG.* THAT'S RIGHT, I WANT YOU TO WRITE THE ENDING FIRST! THAT WAY YOU WILL HAVE YOUR FINAL DESTINATION IN CLEAR SIGHT AND (HOPEFULLY) MAKE WRITING CHOICES THAT DRIVE YOU TO THAT CLIMAX.

NOW GO BACK IN YOUR OUTLINE AND PLANT ONE "CALL-BACK" TO THE FINAL SCENE OR TAG.

13

HOW TO BE FUNNY

By now you're well into writing your script, but you still may have questions about whether you're doing it right. It's sort of like the first time you have sex, and you find yourself pausing mentally in the middle of the action to wonder what the other person is thinking of your performance. (Okay, it's nothing like that. But I got your attention, didn't I?)

You wonder if you are making it funny enough, and if your dialogue and scenes are good enough. Those are natural – if annoying – feelings to have as you write. But there are ways to answer those questions in the affirmative.

So here are some tips to keep you writing and moving forward without second guessing yourself too much.

Free Beats

Every scene has to start somewhere. But it doesn't necessarily have to start where the story picks up.

Your outline should contain the meat and potatoes of what happens in each scene. But you can have a little fun and write an opening beat that gives the scene a unique flavor. Sometimes it's fun to have a short handle or bit of business to launch into the scene. These are called "free beats." And they are often the most fun to write.

So instead of coming up on Leslie Knope at her *Parks and Recreation* desk complaining about traffic in Pawnee, start her off trying to get the office clock to stop ticking so loudly, or trying to catch a fly without killing it. Think of something no one's seen the character do before and see how that character would, in her/his unique way, try to solve a typical problem. What would Phil Dunphy do with a freezer that is too stuffed to keep everything in? How would Larry David (the *Curb* character) react to someone smoking at the next table? How would Molly Flynn (*Mike and Molly*) pick up loose change if her hands are full?

I would advise you to start as many scenes as possible with a free beat. Because they usually aren't related to the story, they may be the first things you look to cut when your first draft runs long. But I bet a few of them make it into your final draft. And it may end up being some of the writing you're most proud of.

Writing Call-backs

You're probably wondering why I had you jump to the end of your script in the last chapter's assignment. Two reasons:

1. I want you to have a clear target for where your script is heading and how to get there in the most direct, economical path.
2. By writing ahead, you may have planted something that can become a call-back.

As you probably know, call-backs are when you, well, call back a joke or reference that happened earlier in your script. They often are some of the strongest jokes you have because they build on something we've already heard. Not every call-back is gold, but if you can do it artfully and with a twist, they usually illicit a laugh out loud even from a hardened professional reader. And they'll appreciate the skill you demonstrate of being able to tie things together that way.

But how do you plan a call-back? The truth is you don't. No one thinks of a joke with the call-back in mind. You come up with the joke and then later think of the call-back... even if it's only seconds later.

Yet there is a way to create the call-back first. That's to write it first. And that's why I had you write the last two scenes so early.

I am hopeful that somewhere in those last two scenes there is something – some line or reference or story turn – that you can now go and plant early in your script so the later mention of it will *become a call-back*. It's simple reverse engineering.

Though I've never written a murder mystery, I bet this is how CSI writers and other mystery writers' work. They probably plant lots of information in their resolution, and work backwards to plant clues earlier in the story. The real killer was trying to make it look like the victim's wife – a chain smoker – was the murderer. And that's why the detectives found her lipstick-stained Marlboro butts in an ashtray at the crime scene in the first act. Of course, later we'll see the innocent wife smoking in a flashback scene and notice the real murder eyeing her as she crushes out a butt. Maybe even see him reaching for the ashtray when no one is looking.

Those clues and evidence are nothing more than call-backs. And they were planted there on purpose, just like those cigarette butts at the murder scene.

Comedy writers do the same thing. We don't always write the end first, but we do go back through our early drafts looking for things we can turn into call-backs. Oh, Ron Swanson insults a

Frenchman in the second act funeral scene? Maybe I can show him dissing french fries in the first act.

Larry David's is going to be cut off in traffic by a smokey polluting city bus on his way to his big date, dirtying his just washed car? Maybe he should rudely cut off a bus himself in the first act.

Sheldon brags about his durable Timex watch on a date with a hot Ph.D. candidate? Maybe Leonard should tease him about his Timex in an earlier scene.

You may or may not find usable lines to turn into call-backs in the scenes you've written so far. But look for them. When you finish each new scene, take a quick read through and see if anything jumps out at you as a potential call-back or set up for a future call-back.

It's a new way of thinking for some writers, but it can be learned. It's a valuable skill to have and to demonstrate in your spec.

Tee-ing Up Jokes

You've seen this technique done a million times and never knew it had a name.

Remember when Lavern and Shirley would say something like, *"Well that's the dumbest thing in the world"* and then Lenny and Squiggy would burst in. And Lavern would say something like, *"I spoke too soon."* That entrance and follow-up line was what we call a tee-ed up joke because it's set up to easily hit out of the ballpark just like a whiffle ball on a batting tee.

It's a form of setup-punch, where the punchline is either an entrance or a twist on an expectation that's been clearly set (tee-ed) up. When done verbally, a joke is tee-ed up by setting up a list of three things (could be two, could be four) that make you think the next thing coming will be similar in nature. But you don't do what's expected, and that's the punch.

This is one of the easiest forms of jokes, because they're so easy to hit out of the park. And frankly, some comedy writers look down on them because of it. But some live by them.

So, while it's formulaic, it's okay to use one or two tee-ups in your spec, so long as they are good versions. 1970s shows like *Lavern and Shirley* did it often and not very cleverly. But *Frasier* did it often and masterfully.

> **Daphne**
>
> There's nothing more exciting than a first date. All those questions which people ask. What's your favorite food? What's your favorite color? If you could come back as any animal, what would it be and why? If you were asked that, what would you say?
>
> **Frasier**
>
> 'Check please' comes to mind.

Here's another, where Frasier tees up his own joke:

> **Frasier**
>
> There's an incredible piece of scientific equipment known as the Tunneling Electron Microscope. Now, this microscope is so powerful that by firing electrons you can actually see images of the atom, the infinitesimally minute building block of our universe. (PAUSE) If I were using that microscope right now, I still wouldn't be able to locate my interest in your problem.

So, look for places to tee up laughs in your spec. They often read well, and if (big if) they are funny, they will demonstrate you know comedy structure and can pay off a setup.

Sight Gags

Of course, visual humor is a key component of any TV comedy. Even the wittiest series like *Seinfeld* or *Frasier* count on a Kramer entrance or a Martin mishap to balance out the verbal jousting.

But just remember that while sight gags *play* funny on camera, they may not *read* very funny in your spec script, no matter how funny it is in your head. Just think about a Kramer entrance on *Seinfeld*. In a script, it might look something like:

Kramer blasts through the door and slides into the room as he almost falls. He comes to an abrupt stop, his head shaking like a bobble-head doll as he collects himself.

Does that read funny to you? It doesn't to me. In fact, they never wrote any of those entrances; they just wrote Kramer enters and Michael Richards did the rest. They didn't try to write his entrances because they simply wouldn't have been funny on paper.

So, before you pepper your script with wordy stage directions and sight gags, ask yourself if this will read as funny as it might play. If the answer is no, take it out. Because long, wordy passages that don't elicit a laugh are the enemy of a good spec script.

Joke-like Substances

There's a saying in comedy writers' rooms: *Is that a joke or a joke-like substance?*

What that means is, is it truly a funny line or does it simply have the structure and timing of a typical joke?

Quite often, even the best comedy writers fall into the trap of writing joke-like substances. You're pressed for a laugh at a certain point in the script, so you write something that follows the rule of three or contains a funny sounding "k" word like cucumber, or uses some other hack phrase, or cliche to try to illicit a laugh. Lines like *"Helloooo?"* or *"Ya think so?"* Or *"Not!"* A rather recent addition to this list is, *"So this is happening."*

Another joke like substance is a pop culture reference that is supposed to be humorous but isn't. If you're referencing Martha Stewart, Elon Musk, Miley Cyrus or any other over-hyped celebrity, forget it. Don't even bother. It won't be funny.

Neither will references to things that happened fifty years ago. Even on well-written shows, I'm constantly amazed when I hear references to *The Twilight Zone, June Cleaver,* or *The Brady Bunch*. Folks, those are 50 and 60-year-old comedy references. They aren't punchlines. They are fossils.

(I know, I know – you're thinking, *But Kevin, you said in the Author's Note that classic TV series are okay to reference.* Yes, they are useful in learning to write a script. They are not useful as punchlines.)

Whatever type of line it is, if it only looks like a joke on paper but doesn't illicit a genuine laugh, it's a joke-like substance and it doesn't belong in your spec. TV shows already have staffs of writers who can turn out that garbage. They want writers who'll come in and turn a new phrase, find a fresh formula, and tap into current references.

Buttons and Blows

In case you didn't know, every scene in your script should have what's known as a "button" or "blow" – a final joke that ends the scene with a bang. (Hence the term "blow" as in blow-up.)

There are people who made a career of being great blow people – the go-to person when the staff needed that button line to end a scene on a big laugh. I've heard that the late Bob Ellison

(*Mary Tyler Moore, Cheers, Wings*) was great at this. It can be a real art form.

Whether you excel at it or not, your script has to – has to – have a blow for every scene. Blows are the bane of every comedy writer's and sitcom staff's existence. But they have to be there. Have to!

There is no one method or easy solution to this writing conundrum. You simply have to hunker down and do it. So, here's a few ways to approach it:

- A call-back. Yes, call-backs are not only valuable between scenes, but they are also a great way to end a scene. IF it is funny. (Notice the big 'if'?)
- A sudden exit or entrance. With the right line, having someone blow into the scene or out of it can often button a scene with energy. *Seinfeld's* Kramer was used this way a lot, or to kick off a scene with a laugh.
- A character return. Like an entrance, an unexpected or unwanted return can elicit a laugh with the right line attached.
- Exasperation. For some reason, ending a scene on a line of exasperation can often feel like a solid ending. But again, only if it's funny.
- Breaking/dropping/ruining something. Or a pratfall. "Live from New York, it's Saturday Night!"
- Bad news.
- Confusion. Ending a scene with someone confused or bewildered is often a viable button, if it's on story and (big if) it's truly funny.

There's an infinite array of others. Usually, the blow is just a great line. However you do it, make sure you've book ended your scenes with an early laugh (the free beat?) and a strong button.

Professional readers will be looking for them and will definitely notice when they are missing in action.

The Best Jokes

This is a pejorative, as there obviously is no such thing as a "best" kind of joke. Funny is funny, right?

Well, in my humble opinion, when it comes to jokes, there is a greater among equals. For me, the best and funniest lines in any script are the ones where the character saying the line doesn't know it's funny.

For instance, in the two Frasier examples above, Frasier clearly is trying to say something funny and knows he is making a joke. They are still funny because they're great lines. But they are very sitcomy "jokey" jokes.

On the other hand, often characters say something in earnest that they don't realize is ironic or dumb or just funny in the context of the situation. They are saying a serious line, but we the viewer/reader laugh at it because of the context of the scene or situation. Here's a couple of examples, again from *Frasier*.

```
                    Frasier

Oh, for God's sake, Niles, just talk to
Maris. Tell her you erred in not
acknowledging her birthday. She's obviously
a little touchy about her age, but it's not
like this is the first time she's turned
forty.
```

Or...

                        Martin

You've been awfully quiet there.

                        Frasier

I'm sorry, Dad.

                        Martin

No, no, don't apologize. It was a
compliment.

Or...

                        Frasier

You refused to take me to see "West Side
Story" on my 8th birthday.

                        Martin

Because of the gangs! Those would be scary
to any kid.

                        Frasier

Even gangs that dance?

                        Martin

Especially gangs that dance!

Or...

```
          Niles

You're letting masculine vanity and hurt
feelings keep you from something other men
can only dream about in their oxblood
leather chairs with the lights out. ... If
you had ever smelled her hair, you'd know
she's worth at least one more try. She is an
angel, and she is goddess, and she is
waiting for you in the bathroom.
```

In each of those examples, the last line – the funny line – was said in earnest. It wasn't meant to amuse the person the line was said to. But it amused us, the third-person fly-on-the-wall viewing the scene from outside.

For me, those are the "best" lines because they are not contrived jokes; they are real. Or at least, they feel real. And good writing is creating the illusion of reality.

Sure, comedies will always have inhumanly witty characters who make amazingly pithy comments all the time. *Friends* had Chandler. *The Mary Tyler Moore Show* had news writer Murray. *Frasier* had Frasier, Niles, and Martin. But real people just aren't that funny in real life, and if you pepper your script with a lot of Woody Allen or Oscar Wilde types, even the best lines will start to feel contrived and "writerly."

So, after you've finished a draft of your script, go through and police it for jokes that are purposely said as jokes. If you have too many of them, try to replace a few with lines that aren't meant to be "jokes" but are still funny in the context of the scene.

Teaching People to Be Funny

There are a lot of comedy pros and writing gurus who will tell you that you can't teach someone to be funny. And that's probably true – most people are either naturally funny or they're not. But you can explain how a scripted laugh line is structured so that people can recognize them and try to duplicate that formula in their own writing.

So, today I taught you how to be funny. Or more to the point, how other comedy writers were funny in the past, and how you can use their time-tested techniques to be successful at it yourself.

Assignment

FINISH YOUR FIRST ACT AND BEGIN YOUR SECOND ACT. (NO REWRITING YET!) REMEMBER, A COMPLETE HALF-HOUR COMEDY SCRIPT SHOULD BE NO MORE THAN 35-PAGES, SINGLE-SPACED. (SCREENPLAY FORMAT.) SO, IF YOUR FIRST ACT RUNS MUCH PAST PAGE EIGHTEEN, YOU ARE PROBABLY GOING TO RUN LONG IN YOUR COMPLETED ROUGH DRAFT.

BUT DON'T GO BACK AND START CUTTING YET.

JUST TRY TO WRITE TIGHTER GOING FORWARD. ONCE YOUR ROUGH DRAFT IS FINISHED, THERE IS PLENTY OF TIME TO COMB THROUGH IT AND CUT OUT THE FAT TO GET IT DOWN TO 35-PAGES (OR SO).

FIRST ACT DONE? GO ON TO THE SECOND ACT. MAKE SURE EACH OF YOUR STORYLINES IS REPRESENTED IN EACH ACT; THAT YOUR DAYS AND NIGHTS LINE UP, AND THAT ALL THE ENTRANCES AND EXITS MAKE LOGICAL SENSE.

BY NOW YOU'VE PROBABLY GOT A GOOD WRITING RHYTHM GOING. ENJOY IT. THIS IS THE MOST FUN PART OF SCRIPT WRITING. WELL, THIS AND THE DAY YOU SELL IT!

14

WRITING FOR READERS

By now you should be well through your rough draft or into your polish, and you should be thinking about how your script will be received.

What you must understand is, each draft has a different audience, and therefore a different purpose. And you need to write each draft to that specific purpose.

Purpose of a Spec Script

A spec script has one purpose: to convince a reader that you can write.

It is not a production draft. It is not a shooting script. It is not the first episode of your original series idea.

It is a sample script. Period.

A million-person audience will never see it. Not even a thousand people. Probably not 100.

You are writing for a limited audience of full-time entertainment industry professionals. Agents, agents' assistants, studio executives, network executives, and producers. That's it.

They are all college educated. Some have advanced degrees. They are all rich or close to it. Only a few are minorities. They are well-read. They are articulate. They are opinionated. They are funny. They know the history of television and comedy better than you. They know the marketplace better than you. They read lots and lots of scripts and know what a good script looks like. They have very little time to spend on your script. As soon as your script annoys them, they'll move on.

And one more very important thing...

...they all *want something* from that script. They want it to advance *their* career. Not yours. Not the actors who will star in it. Not to help humanity and make the world a happier place. They want YOU to provide them with SUCCESS (and money). That's it.

So now that you know that, what are you going to do? You're going to tailor your spec to that audience.

That means:

1. It will look professional. It will have no spelling mistakes or typos. It will use good grammar and proper punctuation. And you won't use an exclamation point unless you need it. (Notice I didn't write "...unless you need it!")

2. It will be funny and clever. Not "ah, I get it" funny. Laugh out loud funny. It won't be laugh out loud funny on every page, because hardly any script is. (And because comedy professionals don't laugh out loud very much. They say, *"That's funny"* without a trace of laughter or a smile. I kid you not.) But you'll try your hardest to make every page laugh out loud funny anyway or contain one ironic or clever concept that people will be intrigued by. Maybe it's a turn of a phrase, a choice you don't see coming, a bit of business

in a scene, or where the scene takes place. But every page should contain something clever.

3. It will be a "fast read." Don't describe a teenager's bedroom in detail when the phrase "world's messiest room" will do. Break up your dialogue. Write in Master Scene format – no camera angles or shots. Don't direct on paper. Make it look fun to read.

4. Don't make the reader work. That means, don't reference *obscure* news events or historical people. A reference to Richard Nixon is okay. A reference to Donald Segretti is not. (If you don't know who Donald Segretti is and are wondering about it, you now understand my point.) Don't show how smart you are by dropping book titles or obscure literary references that the reader isn't likely to know. Frankenstein - good. Mary Shelley - bad. (That, by the way, was an obscure literary joke.)

5. You will give the reader something to think about or feel. The taste should linger in a good way. They should want to tell other people about your script. Or hand it to them.

Writing for Actors

You're not at this stage yet, but let's cover it anyway. Writing for actors means writing for egos. They don't want to read a good script. They want to read a good part.

So, try to give actors fun things to say. Fun things to do. Challenge their range.

Make the character they play really smart. (Actors love to play smart characters. It makes them feel smart by association.)

Give protagonists bad traits. Give antagonists good traits or a sympathetic side.

Don't write girlfriends; write interesting females. A-list

actresses hate playing girlfriends or wives whose only purpose is to be a prop for the male lead.

Make sure your important characters (i.e., lead actors) have something to do in every scene they're in or take them out of that scene.

Give them powerful entrances. They want their character to explode into the story.

Don't put them in scenes with animals or little kids unless the adult gets to shine.

Make each lead a hero to somebody, even if they are not the hero of the story. Tony Soprano was a hero to his wife (most of the time), his kids (sometimes), and his cronies (all the time).

Remove as many parentheticals and actor directions as possible. Let them discover the character and interpret it.

Since we're focusing on comedy in this book, make sure they have laugh lines. Even straight men get laughs. Go watch an old *Newhart* episode. I don't care how many people say that Bob was the straight man, he was getting laughs in every scene.

Remember, that great parts are built on "moments". A line, a joke, a choice. Make sure your lead characters have one or two great moments.

Writing for the Table

This is another script writing step you'll hopefully get to someday. It's an art.

Even though you and the staff have spent a few weeks polishing the script, you'll still get one more pass at it before it goes to the table read. You will want to use that pass to make it table friendly. Here's a few things to keep in mind:

Table reads are auditory (not visual) experiences. Most people will be looking at the script and *listening* to the dialogue. They definitely won't see the action in the stage directions, because it's not happening. So, make your table script more verbal, then revise your shooting script to be more visual.

If you are writing for the table read (day one of the production week), know who will be in the room. You may want to plant an inside joke or reference that you know won't be in the final script just so it gets a big laugh at the table. (And hence makes the overall read go well.) Is this cheating? You bet. Do successful writers do it? You bet.

If one of your actors is bad at cold reading, actor-proof their lines as much as possible. That even means making sure they don't have a line that is broken across two pages. Or that they have to turn the page to find and read a big laugh line. That four second delay while everyone is turning the page can kill a great joke.

That's right – you even need to paginate the script for the best table read possible.

Write funny/witty stage directions. Remember, someone (probably the director) will have to read your stage directions out loud. It's a thankless job, and people tend to read them in monotones, which can squash the energy of the room.

But if you make the person reading the stage directions entertaining, he will give it a better read and you may even buy yourself a few free laughs that can lift the entire energy of the room.

Get your rewrite done as early as possible to get the script to the actors as early as possible. Actors will work with a script if they have it. But if it arrives at their house at 2 a.m. on the night before the table read, they will come in unprepared, and you will end up having to rewrite good stuff because of it.

Taking Notes

No matter how good your script is, the odds are you are going to get network notes. And studio notes. And director notes. And actor notes. And non-writing showrunner notes. And sometimes, wives of all those people notes.

So, here's what you do: you nod, write them down, and say, "Good note."

No explaining what you meant in the script, how you intended it to play, what you were hoping the actor would do with it.

Write. Nod. "Good note."

Then you go back to the writers' room and decide whether it was a good note or not, and what to do if it wasn't.

Quite often, a big note can be addressed with a small dialogue change or addition. Sometimes you'll have conflicting notes, and you can play good cop, bad cop with the note giver whom you disagree with. "I would have taken your note, but I got this conflicting note from so-and-so that forced me to go another way."

And sometimes, yes, you will take a bad note because the person who gave it has that much clout. So, you'll cut a line you love, change a story beat that still feels right, or do something else that takes the episode further away from your original vision.

But you know what? Unless you created the show, are the showrunner, and you have a long track record of success, it's not your show. It's the network's show. And you have to give them what they want to put on the air.

Yes, they should listen to you. Children should do their homework. Lovers should not cheat. Dictators should be benevolent. But we're in the real world. And we're getting paid handsomely to live there. So don't be a diva. Make the change.

The Table Punch-up

Once the actors have taken their first stab at the script, and you've gotten all the notes, it's time to fix what doesn't work.

Usually, assuming the script isn't a total disaster, that means replacing jokes that don't work and adding a few where the comedy is lite.

You'll be tempted to defend jokes that didn't work at the table, but you still think will work on camera. Try not to. The network and the actors expect to see changes, so give them to them.

Writing for Shoot Night

This is a trick that TV writers know. Have a couple of new lines prepared that you can slip in between takes. Here's why.

Audiences laugh at the unexpected. So, once they've seen you film a couple of takes of a scene, they'll know what's coming. But if you surprise them with a new line or two in the third take, they'll howl.

So, all those lines you love that you had to kill after the table read? Keep them in your pocket for tape night. The actors will be so desperate for something fresh, they'll be happy to try that line again. And the audience will be hearing your favorite jokes and be surprised by them. So, the chance of that line scoring big just increased dramatically.

ASSIGNMENT

FINISH YOUR SECOND AND THIRD ACTS AND WRITE YOUR TAG (IF YOU HAVEN'T ALREADY). IF YOU'VE ALREADY COMPLETED YOUR ROUGH DRAFT, RE-READ YOUR SCRIPT, MAKING NOTES FOR YOURSELF, AND START YOUR POLISH.

IF YOU CAN GET YOUR HANDS ON MORE SCRIPTS FOR YOUR SERIES, READ THEM. AT THIS POINT YOU WANT TO BE IMMERSED IN THAT STYLE, FORMAT, AND VOICE. YOU NEED TO BECOME AN EXPERT ON THE SERIES. IT SHOULD BE PULSATING THROUGH YOU LIKE A SONG ON AN ENDLESS LOOP IN YOUR HEAD. ONLY THIS ENDLESS LOOP SHOULD BRING YOU SMILES.

SOMETIMES AFTER COMPLETING A DRAFT, IT HELPS TO TAKE A

FEW DAYS (OR EVEN A WEEK OR MORE) BEFORE YOU GO FROM ROUGH DRAFT TO POLISHING. BUT THAT DOESN'T MEAN YOU STOP WORKING. WHAT I RECOMMEND IS, DECIDE ON YOUR NEXT SPEC HALF-HOUR SCRIPT AND WRITE THE LOGLINE FOR IT. EVEN IF YOU NEVER END UP WRITING THIS SCRIPT, JUST THE ACT OF THINKING ABOUT YOUR NEXT WRITING PROJECT FOR A FEW HOURS OR A DAY, WILL FREE UP YOUR CREATIVITY SO THAT WHEN YOU RETURN TO WORKING ON YOUR CURRENT PROJECT, YOU'LL PROBABLY HAVE A FRESHER, MORE OBJECTIVE TAKE ON IT.

15

HONING YOUR DRAFT

I've talked a bit about writing dialogue already. But since it's such a huge part of half-hour writing, I want to delve a little deeper on the subject.

Whereas movies tend to be about big visuals, dramatic action and actor reactions, televisions shows are more about what the characters are saying than what they are physically doing. I believe that's because in the 1950s and 60s, as the nation moved from going to movies to watching TV, a new way of consuming entertainment emerged. People were no longer bound in a movie seat. They were free to get up from their couch, go to the bathroom, or go to the kitchen for a snack. Housewives ironed, folded laundry, and even vacuumed while watching their favorite daytime soap operas.

Sure, there were also TV dinners which let families stayed glued to their TV sets. (There's a phrase you don't hear anymore.) But between meals, watching TV was often more like listening to TV.

So as people became less visual in their entertainment

consumption and more auditory, the people making the product changed their creative style to match.

What emerged is a visual medium that is really an auditory medium with pictures. TV scripts were designed to be more like radio plays from the 1930s and 40s than screenplays, but with a few big sight gags thrown in to justify having a TV in your home.

That led to an evolution in the way entertainment scripts were developed and produced. Language became the medium for communicating ideas and hooking viewers. And dialogue became king.

At least, that's my theory of how we got here. But regardless of how, good dialogue is the lifeblood of TV comedy. So, let's take a look at what it takes to make your dialogue sing.

Composing Dialogue

Writing funny, crisp dialogue is like writing song lyrics. There's a rhythm and lyricism to it. You have to hear it in your head and sound it out loud. I'm often whispering the lines I'm writing to myself and probably look quite mad when I do it in Starbucks. But you have to hear it and say it to know how it will trip off the actor's tongue. Writing is on some level acting. If you can't say a line without tripping over the wording, don't expect the actors to do it. You want to make your dialogue actor-proof. And you do that by making it writer-proof. With YOU being the writer. If you can say it comfortably in one breath, hopefully a more talented performer will be able to say it, too.

The other way to do it is to count syllables, making sure each sentence has no more than one or two multi-syllabic words. Does that seem constrictive? Go read some of your favorite songs. That's right, read it – find the lyrics online and read them out loud. You'll be amazed at how few words in the song are more than one syllable. Maybe only a handful in the entire song.

In fact, let's test that theory right now. Here are the lyrics to The Beatles tune, *I'll Follow the Sun* (written by John Lennon and Paul McCartney).

ONE DAY, YOU'LL LOOK
TO SEE I'VE GONE
BUT TOMORROW MAY RAIN, SO
I'LL FOLLOW THE SUN
ONE DAY, YOU'LL KNOW
I WAS THE ONE
BUT TOMORROW MAY RAIN, SO
I'LL FOLLOW THE SUN
AND NOW THE TIME HAS COME
AND SO, MY LOVE, I MUST GO
AND THOUGH I LOSE A FRIEND
IN THE END YOU WILL KNOW
OH-OH-OH, ONE DAY, YOU'LL FIND
THAT I HAVE GONE
BUT TOMORROW MAY RAIN, SO
I'LL FOLLOW THE SUN
AND NOW THE TIME HAS COME
AND SO, MY LOVE, I MUST GO
AND THOUGH I LOSE A FRIEND
IN THE END YOU WILL KNOW
OH-OH-OH, ONE DAY, YOU'LL FIND
THAT I HAVE GONE
BUT TOMORROW MAY RAIN, SO
I'LL FOLLOW THE SUN

In that 124-word song, there are only two unique multisyllabic words: "tomorrow" and "follow." And those aren't very hard words to say, either. In fact, most great song lyrics use very simple words.

My point: your dialogue should be just about as speakable as a good song lyric. So go through and turn big words into smaller ones, and compound sentences into simpler ones. Don't write "enunciate" if "say" works as well.

The other thing you want to do is make sure your dialogue "bounces" and "pops." To do that, make sure most of your exchanges are one sentence or less, taking up no more than a line or a line and a half of dialogue.

                    KEVIN 1

        This is a line that pops.

                    KEVIN 2

        Whereas this intricately worded snippet of
        prose is difficult to pronounce, devoid of
        comedic timing, and probably couldn't be
        enunciated by anyone but a professional
        auctioneer.

                    KEVIN 1

        So, keep your lines tight--

                    KEVIN 2

        --and bounce them back and forth--

                    KEVIN 1

        --like a ping pong match.

                    KEVIN 2

        With short, easy phrases--

                    KEVIN 1 / KEVIN 2

        --that pop!

Visual Motifs

Now that we've beaten dialogue to death, let's talk about the visual theme of your script. Yes, a great script is supposed to have a visual theme, or "visual motif." In a movie it could be water, (rain, fountains, puddle splashes, sweat) or sunlight, (creating halos or glaring out an image) or some other visual cue that sets a mood, or conveys a subtextual message. Or, as we found out before, it can be the rings on a tire representing the endless circle of an engagement ring.

In *JFK*, Oliver Stone used sunlight itself to indicate when a clue illuminated the assassination coverup. He would bounce sunshine off a character's head or drown a scene in blinding rays to indicate that this is some major truth you'd better pay attention to.

Lee Harvey Oswald from JFK

Jack Ruby from JFK

Whatever you may think of the historical accuracy of Stone's film, *JFK* is a masterful piece of cinematic storytelling that every script writer should study.

Obviously, sitcom episodes aren't that sophisticated. But you can still use visuals to add depth to your story. Maybe Leslie Knope is out to battle Pawnee's obesity problem. At the top of some scenes, you could have your regulars dealing with a vending machine, cookie jar, soda can, or chewing gum to get convey the theme in visuals.

Or, as was done in the brilliant HBO series *Veep,* Vice President Selina Meyer could try to convince her daughter that, "I know not everything is about *me!*" In a room full of blown-up magazine covers of her face.

So, try to come up with some simple but impactful visual motifs to embed in one of your storylines. Don't be too artsy, but also don't be afraid to be artistic. Good, three-dimensional writing is allowed even in silly half-hour TV comedies.

Subtext

Subtext is what a character is really saying between the lines, and what your story is really about. It can be revealed by a character's words, actions, and reactions, or by a visual motif that you've created to imply the hidden meaning of the story.

For instance, Alfred Hitchcock used to use vertical lines in front of the actors in his shots to subtly suggest the image of prison bars. Here are two shots from *Rear Window.*

Shots from Rear Window *by Alfred Hitchcock (Paramount Pictures)*

This next one is from Hitchcock's *The Wrong Man* (Warner Bros.). If you can't tell, that's a bank teller's cage. But the visual subtext these shots communicate is that of characters caged in by their own actions and circumstances.

There is also a famous shot in one of his films where the shadow of window blinds creates that image over the characters. These images imply a subtext that these characters are all "imprisoned" in their hellish story.

In the case of *The Wrong Man,* the bars foreshadow Henry Fonda's ultimate arrest and imprisonment at the film's end. That visual motif was so powerful that it's been "borrowed" by film makers ever since.

Hitchcock's films are classics in their own right, and writers today would do well to add them to the list of movies they've viewed and absorbed.

Of course, in a half-hour sitcom episode you probably won't get the chance to be that creative with your subtext. Your characters will have to carry the subtext, not in their dialogue but in how they deal with their given situation. Subtext should never be said explicitly by the characters – you don't want a line that states your theme or subtext literally – but you can find creative ways to plant it so it can be understood by the viewer (or reader) as the story unfolds.

For instance, if you are telling a story about *Modern Family's* Cameron Tucker dealing with weight issues, you might put him in scenes where people are constantly eating or snacking. Or if *30 Rock's* Liz Lemon was struggling to make a TGS sketch funny, she might go for a walk in Central Park and see mothers tickling their children and being rewarded with big laughs.

There are also literary techniques like foreshadowing, symbolism, archetypes, etc. But I don't want to get too lofty in a TV comedy writing book. Let's just say that if you can use these devices while staying true to the tone and style of the series, it will make your writing richer and may just make you a richer writer in the process.

Breaking The Rules

The best rule is: don't break any rules. Write your script as close to the format and style of the real show's scripts. That's my suggestion.

Now, if you want to break the rules – hey, maybe you're a creative genius, I don't know – and you're willing to roll the dice on it, do it. The best example is Shane Black. He's a screenwriter who wrote a spec feature script called *The Last Boy Scout*."Black was already a very successful movie writer, but he wanted to hit the jackpot in a spec script auction. So, he sat down and wrote a movie the way he wanted to, including adding a lot of stage directions that normally wouldn't be in a script – and insulting the reader along the way. That's right, insulting the reader! Here's an example from the script:

```
INT. DINGY DRESSING ROOM - NIGHT

Cory and Jimmy are engaged in very
hot sex. This is not a love scene;
this is a sex scene.

Sigh. I'm not even going to attempt
to write this quote-unquote "steamy"
scene here, for several good reasons:

!) Things that I find steamy are none
of your business, Jack, in addition
to which...

2) My mother reads this shit. So
there!
```

Yup, that's really what he wrote. And this stage direction from another page:

Remember Jimmy's friend, Henry, who we met briefly near the opening of the film? Of course you do, you're a highly-paid reader or development person.

Now, I think we can all agree that what Mr. Black wrote is not exactly typical or advisable. Yet the script was riddled with wise-guy asides like this. And it sold for $1,750,000 (which was an astronomical sum in 1990).

Shane Black knew how to break the rules. So did Picasso.

But just remember, even Picasso had to learn the rules before he could turn them on their head.

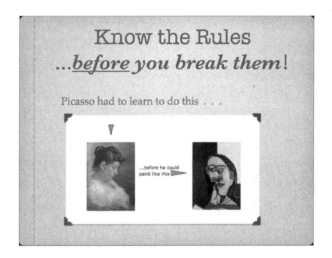

Know the Rules
...*before you break them*!

Picasso had to learn to do this . . .

...before he could paint like this

ASSIGNMENT

READ – *THE OFFICE* PRODUCTION SCRIPT, "THE CARPET" (WRITTEN BY PAUL LIEBERSTEIN) POSTED AT

HTTPS://KEVINKELTON.COM.LINKS

REMEMBER THAT THIS IS A SHOOTING SCRIPT MEANT FOR

PRODUCTION, NOT A SPEC SCRIPT. SO, IT WILL HAVE ADDITIONAL PRODUCTION FORMATTING ELEMENTS THAT YOUR SCRIPT SHOULD NOT CONTAIN. BUT I FIGURE, IF YOU'RE GOING TO READ SCRIPTS, YOU MAY AS WELL READ ONES WRITTEN BY THE BEST IN THE BUSINESS.

WRITING EXERCISE – JUST FOR FUN, FIND A SCRIPT ONLINE (IT CAN BE ONE OF THE ONES AT **KEVINKELTON.COM** OR ANYPLACE ELSE THAT HAS SCRIPTS) AND TRY TO PUNCH UP A COUPLE OF SCENES. YES, EVEN IF IT'S A HILARIOUS, PROFESSIONALLY WRITTEN SCRIPT, TRY TO FIND PLACES WHERE YOU CAN MAKE THE JOKES BETTER OR ADD NEW ONES. THE BETTER THE SCRIPT, THE HARDER IT WILL BE. BUT, LIKE LIFTING WEIGHTS, THE MORE YOU PUT YOURSELF TO THE TEST, THE STRONGER AND BETTER YOU'LL BECOME.

16

SUBMITTING YOUR SCRIPT

For the first 19 chapters, we've talked about one aspect of your TV spec script: the content. Now let's talk about the packaging.

Dress Your Script for Success

No matter how great your script is, if it doesn't *look* professional, forget it. No one will read it beyond a few pages.

Gone are the days when William Goldman could write and sell *Butch Cassidy and the Sundance Kid* without knowing what a movie screenplay looked like. Today, with so much material available for free on the internet, there's no reason your script shouldn't be formatted just like your show's real scripts. And with spell checkers, there's no reason for *thiings likke thys*.

So, proof. Then proof again.

Also, know your show and its characters. In *Modern Family,* is it Lily or Lilly? In *Parks and Recreation*, is it Ann or Anne? (It's the first in both cases.)

Does *Modern Family* use "Talking Heads" or "Interviews"? (Interviews. *Parks and Recreation* calls them Talking Heads.)

What are the actual set names the show uses? Is it?...

```
INT. DUNPHY KITCHEN
```

Or?...

```
INT. PHIL AND CLAIRE'S KITCHEN
```

It's the latter.

Do they write the character name as Cam or Cameron? (Cameron) Do Mitchell and Cameron live in a house, a condo, or a duplex? (A duplex.)

Are *The Big Bang Theory* scripts written in the single-spaced, one-camera format or double-spaced, 3-camera format. (Double-spaced.)

You need to know these details and match them e-x-a-c-t-l-y.

You also need to know how many scenes and how many pages their typical script is. If *New Girl* scripts are around 32-pages and yours comes in at forty, readers are going to go bug-eyed by page thirty-five. And they'll never see your page forty unless you are amazingly brilliant.

However, there are some things in a real script that you absolutely don't want in your spec. You don't add:

- cast lists
- set lists
- production rundowns
- in the case of *The Big Bang Theory,* what they call the "Scientific and Unfamiliar Terms" page

None of these belong in your spec. It goes from title page directly to FADE IN.

Also, your spec script should have a very simple title page with just the series title in bold (no crazy fonts), the episode title,

Written by (your name), and the date of your draft in the bottom right corner Don't write "First Draft." They'll assume it's that. And never ever write "Second Draft" or "Third Draft". Whatever you send out is the first draft, even if you've revised it five dozen times.

If you want to put your contact info (address, phone, email) in the bottom left corner, that's fine. But that's it. Nothing else.

While we're talking about the title page, I suggest you *don't* write "Registered WGA" or any other copyright information. A lot of pro readers consider it the sign of an amateur. And frankly, it's doubtful that someone is going to steal your spec. If they want to, writing "Registered WGAw" isn't going to deter anyone. It's not even a legal copyright.

Do not bold character names or sluglines.

On multi-camera shows, things like sluglines, stage directions, character names and parentheticals are always capitalized, and entrances or exits are always underlined.

On single-camera, single-spaced shows, sluglines and character names are still in caps, but stage directions are in sentence case.

Multi-camera shows use letters to "number" their scenes. If you get through twenty-six scenes, the twenty-seventh is called AA, the twenty-eighty is BB, and so on.

Single camera, single-spaced scripts generally do not use "CUT TO" between scenes. (A few shows break this norm – see which way yours does it.) But if you are writing a multi-camera, double-spaced script, you should write "CUT TO:" and start the next scene on a new page, with a line labeled SCENE B about a third of the way down the page.

Writing Style Choices

The writing style of your script should be consistent and lean. Always use the present tense active voice (Leslie walks into the office).

Don't "direct" the show with too many camera angles. Avoid ANGLE ON or other filmic camera moves.

Don't have characters call each other by their first names any more than is absolutely necessary. Listen to how you talk to your friends and family and see how often you actually use their names – virtually never. So let your dialogue be at least that real.

Never explain something. Don't say, "Leslie first met this character on the third episode of the fourth season, when Lil' Sebastian was buried." If you can't get the info into the dialogue in a natural way, there is probably something wrong with your content. In other words, if you think you need to tell the casual reader what former episode this character or running joke first appeared in, it's too inside to be in your spec script.

Don't leave "orphan" lines at the top of a page. (An orphan is a line of dialogue without a character name at the top.) If you must break dialogue in the middle of a speech, write (MORE) underneath and add (CONT'D) at the top of the next page next to the name of the character still speaking.

Or better yet, use a forced page break and keep the entire speech on one page.

Parenthetically Speaking

As you know, directions for actors are written in parentheticals (WRITTEN LIKE THIS) on their own line in the dialogue.

What you may not know is, most actors hate them. HATE them. On *Boy Meets World*, the wonderfully talented William Daniels was one of those actors, and when I first joined the staff, I was warned by the other writers to use parentheticals in his dialogue at my own risk. Later I saw what they meant. If he saw one in his dialog, his whole body would tense up as he came to that line. And if he saw a second one, he'd break character, look at the writer, and mumble politely but firmly, "No need for you to make acting choices. That's my job." But Bill usually made the right choice...or a better one. So, they weren't necessary.

But there will be times that you absolutely need to use a parenthetical to make sure an ambiguous line isn't misinterpreted. Sarcastic lines often fall into this category. If you must write a parenthetical, keep it very lean and to the point.

Don't write (he glances at Manny as he says). Write (to Manny).

Don't write (she pauses, considering how to respond). Write (beat) or (then) or (pause).

Don't write (laughs reflexively against his better judgment). Write (laughs).

When you go through your script for your second and third pass, look at each parenthetical and ask yourself again if you truly need it. If you think maybe you don't, take it out. It's hard enough to be a writer. Let directors direct and let actors act.

Paper Script or eDoc?

I don't know if there is any one etiquette or answer on this one. So, my suggestion is to ask the person who has agreed to read your script which they prefer.

Some readers like paper because it's easier to read and they can mark it up with a pen and dog-ear pages.

Others will prefer to read your script on their iPad and type their notes right into the doc. This raises another question: what format to send the doc in? If you write in Final Draft and send that out, well, a lot of people don't have Final Draft and your doc won't open or will open in gibberish. Pages isn't compatible with PCs, and Word isn't always a safe bet either. My suggestion is to send a .PDF as your default choice unless they request it in another format.

If you aren't speaking directly to the potential reader, for instance if you are submitting it to an agency or manager, send a hard (paper) copy. Two brads (not one), single-sided (not two-sided – the planet will survive the extra paper in your single-sided script).

If you are submitting it to a studio, network or a show, always send a hard copy. Same for a writing contest – unless they request otherwise, submit it on paper.

Registering Your Script

As I said before, it's pretty unlikely that someone will try to steal your spec. But writers still like to protect their hard work and intellectual property, so let's discuss how.

The two best methods I know are 1) registering it with the Writers Guild of America (WGA) and 2) certified mail it to yourself in a sealed envelope. If you mail it to yourself, don't open it – just store it unopened in a file cabinet and hope you never need it.

The WGA charges non-members $20 to register a script, and it can be done either by mail, online or in person. For more details, see **http://www.wgawregistry.org/webrss/**

A slightly less formal method is simply to email a non-editable .pdf version to yourself or a relative and keep it in your inbox.

Just remember, whether you register with the WGA or mail, or email the script to yourself, all it proves is that on such-and-such date you had that script written. It is not a copyright, and it will still be challenging to prove in court that the plagiarist outright stole your intellectual material. Especially, if they are smart enough to go in and change a lot of things to make it look like their own work.

But sleep well knowing that it's very, very rare that someone steals an entire script. And like a car thief or a house burglar, if they're hellbent on stealing your stuff, they're going to do it, no matter how many deterrents you try to throw in their way.

ASSIGNMENT

Have two trusted friends read your script and give you an honest evaluation. If you're lucky, you have a writer friend or two who can give you some competent, insightful notes. If not, you'll have to rely on your sibling or spouse who watches enough TV to have a decent instinct for what works and what doesn't. Take their notes, don't argue, and then decide which ones you want to address and which you'll ignore. Not every note has to be taken, especially from people who may not be very skilled at script analysis.

When you're done with your rewrites and have a draft you think is ready to show to the world, go out and celebrate! You've just accomplished one of the most difficult creative endeavors. You're brave, you're determined, and you're a success.

You're a writer now. No one can ever take that away from you.

WRITING THE PILOT

WRITING THE PILOT

17

TYPES OF PILOTS

Before I get to telling you what a TV pilot script is, let's start by looking at what is a TV pilot script is NOT.

As a long-time TV writer, I can't tell you how many times someone has said to me, *"My office would make a great sitcom"* or *"My family IS a sitcom."* No, it won't and no it's not. A successful sitcom pilot is not simply a funny premise or work/school/family environment. It is not a collection of oddball characters who walk into a scene and say wacky things.

And a successful pilot script is not a showcase to show what a wonderful writer you are. In fact, in the best scripts, the writer can't be seen in the words or in the produced scenes. Good writing should be invisible. A TV pilot is a performance art, not a written one. It is not about you; it is about the characters and the series.

What a pilot script IS, is a written blueprint that introduces a concept (or "premise") that supports a universal literary theme and the characters who will best illustrate that theme over time.

Let's stop and think about that sentence. A pilot script is a blueprint because it is just the verbal foundation of an overall production. Actors, directors, set designers, casting agents, network executives, and a slew of other key crew members will have their input in the pilot, too. They will interpret your words. They will change them. They will ask you to change them. They will add subtext and tone to the pilot. So, while you may be the writer and executive producer (and in the case of Will Forte or Tina Fey, even the star) of your pilot, you do not own it. It is a collaboration. It is a collective vision. So don't be married to your words. They are just words.

Hopefully well-chosen words. But actors and a crew make a pilot, not just a writer.

There are three types of pilots:

- Premise pilots
- Prototypical pilots
- Hybrid pilots

Let's take a look at each. But before we do, understand that these are not necessarily terms that everyone in the television industry knows. Writers know them, and hopefully network executives and studio development people know them. But your agent may or may not, and your actor friends probably won't. So don't tell your agent you have a great "prototypical pilot" to pitch – she'll probably think you're babbling.

Premise Pilots

A premise pilot is based on a high-concept idea that is relatively unique. People tune in initially because they heard there is a new show about a funny alien, or a high school rock star, or the last man left on earth after a nuclear war and they are curious about how that premise will be pulled off.

But a premise pilot will not work with just a great premise

alone. That's the gimmick or hook that may get viewers to sample it. "Hey, let's check out that new show about the girl who's a high school rock star!" But without a strong, compelling theme and great characters to illustrate that theme every week, the premise will soon grow old and the viewers will lose interest.

Premise Pilots

- Mork & Mindy; Hannah Montana; Last Man on Earth
- lots of backstory
- needs audience buy-in
- not a typical episode
- "Okay, so what's the series?" syndrome

The theme of *"Hannah Montana"* was that being famous isn't always all it's cracked up to be, so it's okay just to be a normal dorky teenager, just like you (the viewer).

That theme, and how well it was executed, was why tweens came back to watch every week. Yes, they wanted to see what it would be like to be famous in high school, to have everyone love you and be fabulously rich and successful. But they liked seeing that being just a regular kid with regular problems was pretty cool, too.

Premise pilots need a lot of backstory. We need to know that Miley's dad is a great song writer, that musical ability runs in their family, and that he doesn't want his teenage daughter to give up the innocence of her teenage years.

In *Mork and Mindy*, we need to know that Mork has been sent to Earth to study humans and human emotions, and that he has been chosen for the mission because humor is not permitted on his planet. We also learn early in the pilot that Mindy just broke up with a lecherous boyfriend, so there is a place in her life for a funny, charming man who will treat her well.

It's also important that the audience buy into the premise. They have to suspend belief and accept that the world has come to an end except for a handful of survivors in the midwest, that the head of a New Jersey Mafia family is a neurotic henpecked husband and dad who is prone to fainting spells, that a world-famous rock star can take off her wig and go completely unrecognized by everyone she knows. It doesn't have to make complete sense. As anyone who ever saw Superman knows, it was just a pair of glasses that made Clark Kent totally indistinguishable from the Man of Steel. But viewers have to buy it in the context of the world of the pilot. If they want to suspend their beliefs because of the fun they will have each week watching that world and those characters, they will gladly buy almost any wild premise. Even that a lowly delivery man who looks like Kevin James could be married to Leah Remini.

Prototypical Pilots

A Prototypical pilot, on the other hand, is a day in the life of the characters. It doesn't start with something major or unusual happening in their lives, like moving or starting a new job or an alien landing in their backyard. If produced properly, the pilot story could just as easily have been the fourth episode or the tenth. We are just entering a world that is already in progress. Prototypical pilots usually need only a minimal amount of backstory.

Prototypical Episode

- minimal amount of backstory needed
- a day in the life
- could be 1st, 4th or 10th episode shown
- readers/viewers immediately "get" the series

"*Veep*" is a great example of a prototypical pilot. When we meet Selena Meyer and her staff, it's not the first day of her term as vp. They've all been on the job for a while and all know each other. We just meet them on a stressful day in their lives, which turns out to be just like every other day in their Washington, D.C. power world. No one new shows up; nothing changes in her job or their work situation. The pilot could just as easily been shown several weeks later in the run and it would have played just as well. (Although the episode did kickoff some storylines that were continued into the first season.)

Hybrid Pilots

In a Hybrid pilot, we enter a pretty typical world but see it for the first time through the eyes of someone new who is entering that world with us. Someone new shows up at the workplace or in the neighborhood/apartment, building/school, and in the process of everyone meeting them, we get to meet them and everyone else. It's a hybrid of a premise pilot and prototypical pilot because it does require an inciting incident to get things going. But it's not a high-concept hook, it's just a new face or new state of things that slightly changes the daily lives of the people in the show.

Hybrid Pilot

- Introduces an existing world through new players
- someone new shows up at the workplace
- something changes in people's daily lives
- usually one character is a "window" into this new dynamic or world
- some backstory, but less than one act's worth

In the pilot of *Brooklyn Nine-Nine* everyone was already working at the Nine-Nine except Captain Holt, who took over the precinct that day. But his entrance into their world didn't change their world or throw their lives in a whole new direction – they were still cops working in the same place. It was just one of the storylines and the device that the writers used to introduce the characters to him and, hence, introduce them to the viewers.

In the next chapter, we'll talk about the elements of a successful pilot and the elements that the writer controls.

ASSIGNMENT

WRITE – A SHORT (3-5 PAGES) SAMPLE SCENE (NOT TO BE USED IN YOUR PILOT) THAT PLACES YOUR LEAD CHARACTER IN A SITUATION THAT HAPPENS TWO YEARS BEFORE YOUR SERIES BEGINS. PLACE THEM IN AN INTERESTING SITUATION WITH AT LEAST ONE OTHER CHARACTER (AGAIN, SOMEONE NOT IN YOUR SERIES) AND REVEAL THREE THINGS ABOUT HIS OR HER PAST THAT HELPS FORM THEIR PERSONALITY. USE THIS EXERCISE TO DISCOVER YOUR LEAD CHARACTER.

WRITE – THE THEME OF YOUR PILOT IN A SHORT, CRISP DECLARATIVE SENTENCE. TRY NOT TO BE VAGUE OR TOO GENERAL. COME UP WITH A SPECIFIC, HOPEFULLY UNIQUE THEME THAT YOU WISH TO EXPLORE THROUGH YOUR CHARACTERS.

18

THE PITCH

Once you have the idea for your pilot that you like and believe has "legs," you need to focus on the pitch for it. Yes, even if you're going to write the entire script before you try to sell it, you need to know your pitch. Why? Because it's the best way for you to truly understand what your pilot is about.

A successful pilot has many key elements, the script being just one. But if the script isn't right, nothing else will make it work.

The script has to be virtually flawless. You have 32-pages to sell a reader on the concept, the characters, the world, the theme, the tone, the humor, and the point of view. It's a lot to do in very little space. And it all has to be there.

The Elevator Pitch

So how do you create a pitch that will lead to a workable pilot? Most people make the mistake of starting with a premise: two guys who have to dress in drag to live in an all-girls dorm; the writing staff of a TV show; a doctor married to a female football referee.

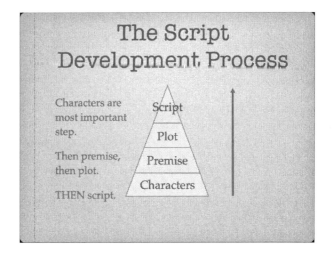

Wrong. The most important aspect of your show – and therefore your starting point – is *character.* A TV series is first and foremost about people – not where they work or what they do.

Character should determine premise.

Premise should determine plot.

Plot should determine script.

But this is how too many writers approach it...

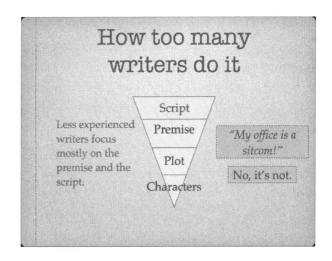

So yes, Seth McFarland probably thought, "I'd like to do a

satire of a typical family sitcom." But he needed Peter before he could know the full world and dynamic of the show.

Knowing who Peter was determined what kind of characters (family members) he'd be living with, what he did for a job, who his friends were, and how the show would skew traditional TV comedies. For example, until you know that the dad is a self-absorbed, nihilistic, non-compassionate, misogynistic ass, you can't find Meg or Chris, who are both the product of Peter's flawed parenting skills.

And without Michael Scott, you wouldn't have a Dwight Schrute to kiss up to him, or a Stanley to totally disrespect him, or a Jim who is the intellectual and charismatic superior to him, or a Toby who has to clean up all of Michael's managerial screw-ups.

But if you'd put Michael Scott in another setting, you would probably have very different characters surrounding him.

Pitching the Theme

What all that adds up to is, that a great pitch doesn't try to sell someone on a premise or a hook. It tries to sell them on the why of your script or pilot idea – the theme.

If you can sell the intended listener/buyer on WHY they should care about your script or pilot idea, you are half-way to the goal line.

Watch the video interview with Barry Kemp as he explains how he came up with the character and premise for the ABC series, *Coach*.

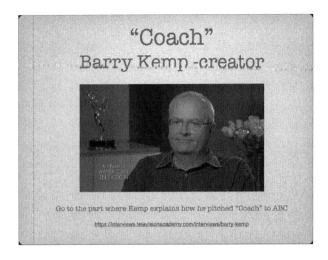

"Coach"
Barry Kemp -creator

Go to the part where Kemp explains how he pitched "Coach" to ABC
https://interviews.televisionacademy.com/interviews/barry-kemp

Here's the link: http://www.emmytvlegends.org/interviews/people/
barry-kemp

Go to Shows – Coach – Barry Kemp on how *Coach* came about.

Listen to his story about how he came up with the idea for the
Hayden Fox character, and how he sold it to the ABC development executives.

What's interesting is that he didn't start his network pitch
with: "*Here's a show about a college football coach and all the crazy characters he works with.*" He started it with a recognizable and univer-
sally sympathetic character who determined the premise and
theme of the series. From the way he describes the meeting, it
seems he sold *Coach* by selling its theme. In my opinion, it is a
master class in TV pitching.

And by the way, try to listen to as much of this interview as
you can. Barry Kemp is a great showrunner and his stories are a
master class in how to create great television.

I want you to come up with a five-sentence pitch of your pilot
idea, focusing on a theme and a character. Do not tell us his job
or the setting of the series until you've told us those two key
elements. Push yourself to really define and know WHO you are

writing about. It will make the WHAT that much stronger. Only then do I want to hear your hook or setting. It may feel ass-backwards but if you can tell it that way, you will be better prepared to write it.

Write your pitch and practice it a few times. Since this is a book and not a classroom, we don't have the luxury of pitching our ideas to each other out loud. But if you tell it to your friends and family, and get their feedback to hone it, you will be much closer to being ready to write the script that executes that vision. It also helps to know the locale of your series (east coast vs. west coast vs. middle America, major city vs. rural vs. bedroom community, etc.) and the platform you hope to see the show delivered on (network TV, paid cable, free cable, streaming, webisodes, etc.) because each of those will dictate the content and format in some way.

The Pilot Pitch

- catchy
- succinct
- funny
- succinct
- intriguing
- short ... concise ... tight ... succinct

In my live classes, I have students practice this skill by picking a famous show and pitching it to us as if we'd never seen it before. Sometimes they nail it. Sometimes they don't. But the exercise is very educational. So, I suggest you try it with a couple of shows you like. See if you really know what a successful series is about. It will help you understand your own pilot much better, and maybe help you avoid some mistakes you might otherwise make.

ASSIGNMENT

DEVELOP YOUR SERIES PITCH AND PRACTICE PITCHING IT OUT LOUD TO ANYONE WHO WILL LISTEN. HONE IT. TIGHTEN IT. PUNCH IT UP. THE BETTER YOU KNOW IT, THE BETTER YOU WILL KNOW THE PILOT SCRIPT YOU ARE ABOUT TO WRITE.

19

INVENTING NEW CHARACTERS

I'm often asked: how do I create authentic, three dimensional supporting characters? The answer is simple: I don't think of them as "supporting characters."

Remember, every character you create is the LEAD character in his/her world. Do you think of yourself as a supporting character in your brother's or spouse's world? Of course not. Most people are obsessed with themselves — thinking about their problems and how to navigate their lives. So should your cast of characters. Even the snooty maitre 'd at the restaurant your leads are eating at has his own life and his own problems that exist for him regardless of your lead's dinner reservation. They don't know that they are merely there to keep your lead from bumping into her ex. They think they are there to do their job shift, and your series lead is a supporting character in their world.

If you look at the story from each character's perspective as the LEAD in that particular plot line, you will be forced to see them in more than one dimension. (more than just servicing the series lead) You're more likely to find human flaws and quirks that will make them more interesting. Look at George Constanza from *Seinfeld*. He was interesting enough to be a lead and sort of became one when Larry David took that character and based his *Curb Your Enthusiasm* character on him. Whatever type of pilot you write, each of the people working in the workspace, living in the house, or going to the school should feel like the lead of their storyline.

Series supporting characters like *The Office's* Jim and Pam, or *Veep's* Mike McClintock become more "real" and more interesting as the shows' creators give them more and bigger storylines to carry.

Devices (Not Plot Devices)

In a pilot, your real estate is limited, and you have to establish characters quickly and precisely. That's why I always loved the free payphone device in the *Taxi* pilot — it let us get to know something about three characters in a quick yet very creative way —by seeing who they'd call if they could call anyone anywhere in the world.

In the pilot for *Everyone Loves Raymond*, we learn a lot about Ray's mom, Marie, from her reaction to his gift of a subscription to the Fruit of the Month Club. Her unexpectedly harsh, negative reaction and the reasoning behind it tells us so much about Marie that mere quips to Ray or Debra could never convey.

In movies, they say "character is action." In half-hour TV, character is "reaction." You rarely get the chance to put a sitcom character in a life altering situation that forces them to act. But you can put them under stress and see how they react. Find little ways to test your supporting characters. What will they do if the boss suddenly talks to them? What if their lover gives them bad news? How do they react to nasty people or stressful demands?

As I mentioned before, a good writing exercise is to put your supporting characters on a losing streak at a Vegas craps, or blackjack table, or stuck in an elevator with an annoying stranger to see how they react under pressure. Come up with your own highly stressful situation and put them in the thick of it. You might learn about your character and maybe come up with a scene you can actually use at some point.

Remember, don't create coworkers or "friends" of your lead character just to service your lead. I often see the "make-up lady" in a script about a TV start or the dutiful assistant in a workplace comedy, yet all they do is ask the lead questions and provide basic exposition. They have no real life of their own in the script. They are just there to be a sounding board. That's bad writing.

To avoid that, give every character a problem (conflict) at the top of the script – some task or anger that they are already dealing with when we meet them. Then, let them work through it while they are interacting with the lead and her/his conflict. Conflicted, angst-ridden characters are interesting characters. Characters having a nice, typical day are not.

Lastly, ask yourself what storylines this character would carry if the pilot goes to series. Not just a quick premise, but how would that character surprise the viewers and "grow" in that situation? Where will they be after thirteen or twenty-four episodes? How will their relationship with the series lead grow or fray? If you can arc out each character's life to see how they will grow over a year or so, you will probably create more interesting, believable characters that will grow on your audience as well.

Character Warehouses

Whether you're writing a TV spec, a pilot, or a screenplay, you will at some point come up against the problem of developing a new, original character. I've always done it by simply writing and finding the character as I go, then I go back and lay in any quirks or traits that I discovered later in the process.

But some writers prefer to develop their characters before they start scripting. Many will write short or lengthy bios and backstories about their character. I didn't much like that exercise, as I found it tedious, and it felt like busy work.

However, there are some cool ways to discover your character on paper without simply writing bios that will never be used in your script. One idea is simply to find a real person and base it on him/her. The challenge of that, of course, is that you may not know anyone who is like the character you want to write. Maybe he's a martial arts expert, or a sexual cad, or a rich adventurer - and you don't know anybody that remotely fits that type. So where do you find interesting, unique, believable, and compelling characters to write about? Sure, you can sit down and make them up – write a 3-page bio and take days thinking up every nuance of their history and unique qualities. Or you can find them in the real world. But how? After all, you only know so many friends/relatives/coworkers and most of them probably aren't all that interesting.

Well, did you know that there are websites that store millions of character bios? These free websites let you search for types of people and skim through them to read all about their likes and dislikes, their hobbies, their education, careers, physical attributes, their past relationships, religious and political beliefs.All the traits that go into great characters. Do you know what these massive *character warehouses* are called? They're called **online dating sites**.

That's right, you can go to Match, Plenty Of Fish, OK Cupid, and other dating sites and read their profiles for free. You can even search for a specific type of character.

Online Dating Profiles

Need a highly educated, over forty Asian woman who likes to cook and sing karaoke?

There are thousands of them! And their bios will jog your

creative juices and give you plenty to work with.

Of course, as you write the script, you will adapt the character and add or change details. But you saved yourself a lot of writing and you may even find a few things about the real person that you wouldn't have thought of if you tried to write their bio from scratch.

The same is true for Facebook pages, though they are not as fully developed.

And though I've never tried this, I suppose you could even write to the person and tell them you're a screenwriter researching a script, and you spotted his/her bio and thought they'd make a cool character. Then you can ask a question or two to see how they talk and think. Some people may not respond, but I bet a fair amount would, and would probably be tickled to think someone is writing about them.

So, when you're fleshing out your original characters – be they for a pilot script or just day players in your *Big Bang* spec – do a little online fishing of your own and let real, living, breathing people write your fictional character bios for you.

ASSIGNMENT

WATCH – THE *TAXI* PILOT, LOOKING FOR THEMES AND HOW THE WRITERS CREATED CHARACTERS AND DEVICES TO SUPPORT THE THEME. ALSO COMPARE TO SEE HOW THE DAN HARMON STORY STRUCTURE PARADIGM (ABOVE) WORKS IN THIS SCRIPT. HERE ARE A COUPLE OF LINKS THAT MAY WORK:

HTTP://WWW.IMDB.COM/VIDEO/HULU/VI2332077337/

OR...

HTTP://WWW.CBS.COM/SHOWS/TAXI/VIDEO/1799619214/
TAXI-LIKE-FATHER-LIKE-DAUGHTER/

(HINT: IN TERMS OF USING DEVICES TO SUPPORT THE THEME,
THE PAY PHONE AND THE FATHER-DAUGHTER SCENE ARE WHAT
I'M TALKING ABOUT. WATCH HOW THE WRITERS USE THOSE
TWO DEVICES TO REVEAL CHARACTER. ALSO, NOTE HOW
EVERYONE IN THE GARAGE IS DEFERENTIAL TO ALEX. IT SHOWS
THAT HE IS SOMEONE TO BE WATCHED, AS IF THE SERIES
CREATORS ARE TELLING VIEWERS, "PEOPLE LIKE HIM SO I
SHOULD TOO.")

DEVELOP – YOUR PILOT'S A AND B-STORIES, WITH AN
INCITING INCIDENT, AT LEAST THREE ESCALATIONS, AND A RESO-
LUTION FOR EACH. MAKE SURE EACH STORY DISPLAYS AN ASPECT
OF YOUR THEME.

20

ACT BREAKS VS. AD BREAKS

After teaching this subject for many years, I realized that there is quite a bit of confusion regarding the difference between act breaks and TV commercial breaks. In all the years I'd been teaching TV writing courses, it hadn't really dawned on me that TV scripts have been using the wrong terminology for decades. Thereby confusing new writers who may think that TV commercial breaks are truly act breaks. They are not. So, here's some additional instruction around that issue.

First, let's step back and understand that what we are talking about is writing *theory*. Like any theory in any discipline, there will be counter-theories and differing views. Most screenwriting instructors teach a three-act structure but not all. Some try to put their own spin on it, and some are just contrarians. But understanding act structure is imperative for a successful writer.

On the other hand, act breaks are generally not something audiences understand or care about. When you watch a movie, you don't care if the writer thought it was a three act or four act or fifteen act script. All you care about is, if you like it or not. So, when we talk about breaking a story into acts, it is a *writers' device* that generally has little bearing on the audience.Unless you don't understand how to structure your story by acts, in which case *it will have a bearing on your audience* because they will viscerally know something is wrong. The pacing and balance feels "off." They'll say it lagged in the middle or was too choppy and quick someplace else, or it "had no ending." That has to do with act structures.

Now let's get into the theory as I teach it.

A classic story has a three-act structure. That's because every plot has a beginning (Act 1), a middle (Act 2), and an ending (Act 3). You can get fancy but that is the basic molecular structure of any story. This is true whether you are watching a movie, a TV show, a one-act play, a two-act play, or a five-act play like most of Shakespeare's works. Even a (good) one-act play has a beginning, middle, and end. It just doesn't stop for audience intermissions along the way.

But that is very different than the television *commercial break*, which TV scripts mis-label as the end of an "act" and the beginning of the next act.

So, when you talk about television "act breaks," don't think of them as acts in the writing sense. TV executives and producers at some point adopted the term "act break" instead of commercial break. But don't mix them up. They can coincide but not necessarily.

Case in Point: Sometimes a TV episode has three commercial breaks (one after the teaser, one after "act one" and one after "act two" just before the tag) when it first runs on a network. But when it reruns in syndication, the cable channel adds two more commercial breaks to make more money. Did that story suddenly become a five-act plot? Of course not.

So do not mistake commercial breaks for act breaks in the writing sense. TV "acts" are usually structured to have a beat of higher tension or escalation right before the break, which is a writing technique used to hook viewers to come back after the commercials. But it is my opinion that you'd be better off thinking of your story as a three-act structure, and then finding the proper commercial breaks for your script's "Act Breaks" after the story is laid out.

Now, is each act structured exactly the same? No. A first act introduces characters, premise, time, and location -- what some writers call "the world of the story." It may contain a major twist or obstacle, but generally it is more about establishing the story than advancing it. The end of the first act is where the action jump-starts, with what writers call the first plot point. In a movie that is generally around page twenty-five (give or take a few pages). In a half-hour, single-spaced TV script, it could be around page 5-8 (give or take a few). The second act is built on rising tension and obstacles that keep the main character from achieving his/her goals. Screenwriters may use terms like "mid-point," "pinch points," "rising action," "confrontation," "crisis" -- and probably a hundred other terms that are offshoots of those. Here's a pretty good explanation of it:

https://www.studiobinder.com/blog/three-act-structure/

The movie *Rocky* is a textbook example of the three-act structure, and I strongly recommend you watch it again just to study its structure.

- Act 1: we meet Rocky, his world, and his problem: he's a nobody and no one respects him. The act ends with a big twist/escalation: Rocky the nobody is going to be fighting Apollo Creed for the heavyweight championship of the world!
- Act 2: training for the big fight. It's filled with obstacles, complications, and escalations, both in his

training and in his personal life. The act ends with a
big twist/reversal: even though he's trained incredibly
hard and is in the best shape of his life, the fight is just
a show, and he's being set up to lose.

- Act 3: the big fight, ending with a satisfying resolution:
Rocky loses but just barely, beating the bejeezus out of
Creed along the way, and in "going the distance" he
wins the world's respect and attains his personal goal
and self-satisfaction.

Again, you will probably find other writing "gurus" who will
have their own theories and slants. But for the purposes of this
book and the pilot you are working on, I'd like you to think of
your STORY in a three-act structure and your SCRIPT in whatever commercial break structure you want your series to have.
They may be the same, or maybe not. But you, as the writer and
architect of this script, need to know where your act breaks are,
just like an architectural engineer needs to know where his
support beams are.

Otherwise, your story may come crashing down around you.

ASSIGNMENT

WRITE YOUR PILOT SCRIPT FROM THE OUTLINE, USING THE
TECHNIQUES YOU LEARNED IN THE FIRST PART OF THIS BOOK.
FROM NOW ON, WHENEVER YOU WRITE A TV SCRIPT, SCREEN-
PLAY, OR STAGE PLAY, YOU CAN APPLY THIS BASIC PROCESS TO
GUIDE YOU ALONG.

EVENTUALLY, YOU WILL DEVELOP YOUR OWN TRICKS, SHORT-
CUTS AND PROCESSES THAT MAY SUPPLANT SOME OF MINE.
THAT'S FINE. WHATEVER WORKS FOR YOU IS YOUR PROCESS.
I'VE GIVEN YOU THE FOUNDATIONAL SKILLS AND HOPEFULLY THE
INSIGHTS YOU NEED TO LAUNCH YOUR SCRIPT WRITING CAREER.
NOW IT'S UP TO YOU TO BUILD ON THIS FOUNDATION, TAKE THE
PROCESS AND THE CRAFT TO NEW HEIGHTS, AND SHARE THOSE

SKILLS SOMEDAY WITH YOUNG WRITERS. BE KIND TO THEM AND KIND TO YOURSELF.

WRITING ISN'T ALWAYS A JOY. BUT THE SATISFACTION OF FINISHING A SCRIPT AND GETTING POSITIVE FEEDBACK CAN BE ONE OF LIFE'S GREAT LITTLE JOYS IF YOU ALLOW IT TO BE. I LOVE BEING A WRITER. I HOPE YOU DO, TOO.

WRITING THE SCREENPLAY

WRITING THE SCREENPLAY

21

BASIC FILM STRUCTURE

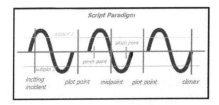

Yes, this is predominantly a book on television writing. But since we're already here, I might as well talk a bit about writing the comedy screenplay. Sure, I could fill a whole book on that topic. But I'll leave that to the so-called screenplay gurus.

Here, I'll just share with you a few tricks that I've culled from those greats as well as my own theories based on my experience writing screenplays. Though I'm best known for TV, I have written my share of feature-length scripts, some that I was hired to write or rewrite and others written on spec that were optioned by movie studios. None were ever produced. If they had been, I'd be richer (and more famous) than I am. But each had its fans, and I'd like to share the same concepts I used to write them with you to help launch your first (or second or third) screenplay, if that's something you want to try. So let's get into it.

I'm not going to coach you to write *Casablanca* or *Kramer vs. Kramer*. This is a comedy writing book, so I'm going to focus mostly on film comedies. (Though I'll sometimes cite a movie drama as well.) What I am going to teach you is how to forge a solid, functional comedy story that will hold up from page 2 to page 112. Anyone can write page one. Anyone can write a happy ending. It's what you do between them that gets your script optioned or tossed in the reject pile.

Learning from the Best

If I was teaching physics, you wouldn't expect all the theories I teach to be my own. You'd want to learn about Galileo, Isaac Newton, Einstein, Madam Marie Curie, and Richard Feynman. Maybe a little Stephen Hawking.

If I was teaching math, you wouldn't want to learn my own equations. You'd want to become versed in Archimedes, Pythagoras, Carl Gauss, and again, Isaac Newton. If we were studying art - which in a way, we are - you'd want to learn the theories and techniques that made Picasso and DaVinci great.

I'm not going to pretend that I'm a movie guru. Instead, I'm going to analyze what the great screenplay gurus know and teach, and share the essence of that with you in a short time span.

What I'm about to explain is borrowed from the teachings of Robert McKee, Syd Field, John Truby and Dr. Linda Seger, as well as the works of several top-notch screenwriters.

Much of the craft of writing a comedy movie is the same as the techniques I taught in the television section of this book. So, I won't repeat them here. Instead, I'll focus on film structure and its relationship to character, the two elements that make or break a screenplay.

The movies I'm going to be referencing quite a bit along the way are *The Hangover* (written by Jon Lucas and Scott Moore), *Rocky* (by Sylvester Stallone), *Airplane!* (by Jerry Zucker, Jim Abrahams, David Zucker), *The Holdovers* (by Jon Lucas and Scott Moore), and *Anchorman: The Legend of Ron Burgundy* (by Adam McKay and Will Ferrell), with quick references to a handful of others. So, you may want to see if you can stream a few of those films to refresh your memory before reading on. It'll come in handy when I get into the nitty-gritty.

And always remember: we are not writing a movie to be watched. We are writing a *screenplay* to be read. They are very different things. Charlie Chaplin's *City Lights* or Peter Seller's *The Party* are classic film comedies. But those scripts wouldn't get you an agent today. Today's comedy scripts need to read well, be easily digestible, and seem marketable.

"Seem" being in the eye of the beholder, because no one knows for sure what is a marketable movie and what is a very expensive box office dud. As William Goldman famously wrote in his book, *Adventures In The Screen Trade,* "Nobody knows anything."

What he meant is, movie studio executives and other self-appointed cinema experts may think they know what will sell and be a hit. But it's all intuition and educated guessing. All you as a writer can do is provide them with a professional, well-thought-out screenplay and hope that someone wants to bet on it.

So How Do I Start?

The same way you started your TV scripts: with an idea and a batch of blank 3x5 index cards. Once you have a general idea for your beginning-middle-end plus some basic characters, start jotting down scene ideas on cards. One scene per card. Since a screenplay runs about 100-110 pages (give or take) and movie scenes run between 30 seconds to two-and-a-half minutes (give or take), you'll want to have around 50 cards with a few scene details on each one before you go to writing your beat sheet.

Once you hit 50 cards (more or less), take a breath. Look at it. Fifty cards is a nice pile. Weigh it in your hands. It will feel like a full story and you'll feel like you're holding a movie in your fingers. Spend a few days (or more) adding thoughts to each card, adding cards when you think of a new scene, moving them around, laying them out on the floor or a tack board to analyze the flow and visually "see" the movie play out in your mind.

Obviously, your movie beat sheet is going to be quite a bit longer than a TV beat sheet, and your outline (in movies, they call it a *treatment*) will be much longer as well, maybe 20-40 pages. Again, give or take.

Once you have a treatment that makes sense, you'll drop it in an empty Final Draft doc (or whatever script writing software you're using) and start morphing it into screenplay format and scenes. You'll probably find yourself inventing new scenes as you go and adding transition scenes where necessary to bridge the gaps. You'll just have a feel as to when you need a transitional moment or need to add something that didn't pop into your mind while writing the treatment.

The format is mostly the same as the one we used for television. See the *Formatting the Half-hour TV Script* link on my website for all the technical jargon. Better yet, pick up a few screenplays of real movies in your genre and study them. Copy their format. Match their look, pacing and style. These are scripts that got made. You can't go wrong modeling your screenplay after successful ones.

Plotting

Of course, a movie plot is going to be a lot longer and more complex than a half-hour sitcom script. But the critical elements are fairly similar.

Let's start with plotting. Plot is not just a sequence of events. A movie plot is a linear sequence of *related events*, one causing the next. Remember the dominos example I used earlier? Movies use the same concept, just a lot more dominos, usually knocking each other down in a more complex pattern.

That pattern may include flashbacks, non-sequential scenes, and other writing devices that break the A to B to C conventions of chronological storytelling.

But regardless of the tricks used, a good story is linear and connected, even when told in flashback (as in *Annie Hall*) or fragmented (as in *Reservoir Dogs*) or non-sequential (as in *Pulp Fiction*). What seems arbitrary to the viewer is really linked in a logical, linear progression by the writer. So, the final product makes sense to the viewer even though it was laid out in what at first appears to be an illogical order.

Basic Structure

A good story shows a character in conflict with the world in a way that motivates him or her to find a solution. How they get to that solution is your story structure – the *map* of your movie.

The basic structure of a movie generally has eleven story points. They are the:

1) inciting incident (often by page 10)
2) plot point 1 (page 22-25)
3) first act break (page 25-30)
4) pinch point (page 45)
5) midpoint (page 60)
6) second pinch point (pg75)
7) rising tension/reversal (page 75-85)
8) second act break - plot point 2 (page 85-90)
9) maybe another pinch point (page 90-100)
10) climax (page 100-110)

11) resolution (page 110-115)

Of course, those page numbers are approximations. Your polished draft may only be 101 pages or it could be up to 125, and the plot points may slide up or down depending on the overall length.

Remember, I said "generally." Every rule has its exceptions, and for every screenplay writing rule, you can probably find five great movies that break that rule.

For instance, in *Rocky*, the inciting incident comes late in the first act, when Apollo Creed's scheduled opponent breaks his hand in training and can't be ready in time for the fight date. So, Apollo has to find a new opponent for his big Bicentennial fight card. That ends up being Rocky. If the first opponent hadn't inured his hand, there would never have been a matchup between Rocky and Apollo. That is why the unseen opponent cracking a finger while training is the inciting incident for the entire movie. (And movie series.)

But though we use the terms "inciting incident" and "plot points," they are not necessarily singular points. Movies are told in sequences – units of action (scenes) that tie together to make an act and a plot.

The inciting incident in *Rocky* is an off-screen scene of the opponent breaking his thumb, leading to a scene in which Apollo settles on Rocky as his replacement, leading to a scene where the fight promoter tells Rocky he's going to be fighting for the heavyweight title. That is a sequence of scenes that establish the movie's conflict and obstacle (Rocky must fight and beat the undefeated champ, Apollo Creed).

Sometimes a plot point is a moment, sometimes it's a sequence. Yet all climaxes are sequences. Think of that title fight in *Rocky*. It's a sequence of rounds that lead to the conclusion of the boxing match and the judges' decision. So, don't let the word "plot point" confuse you. Your plot point may well be several scenes or a sequence.

For an example of basic screenplay structure, let's look at the brilliant comedy film, *The Hangover*. Here is its structure as I break it down.

The Hangover

- **inciting Incident** - Doug invites future brother-in-law Alan on his bachelors' weekend trip
- **plot point** - once in Las Vegas, the guys toast Doug and begin drinking
- **act break** - fade to black
- **act two** - they wake up hungover, with no memory of the prior evening
- **pinch point** - Doug is missing! What happened to him? They are all so hungover, no one can remember. So, to get the answer, they have to recreate the night
- **midpoint** - they learn that Doug's been kidnapped
- **pinch point** - Alan has to win the money needed to buy Doug back from his kidnappers
- **rising tension** - trading the money for Doug
- **reversal** - they got the wrong "Doug"
- **act break** - time is running out, and they're screwed
- **act three** - out of options and time, Phil has to call Doug's fiancée Tracy and tell her the wedding is off
- **pinch point** - Stu suddenly realizes, "I know where Doug is!" They find him locked on the roof of the hotel
- **rising tension** - now that they have Doug, they need to get him back home in time for his wedding
- **climax** - the wedding sequence, and all is well again in their world
- **resolution** - Alan shows them photos from the night before, filling in the missing holes in their memory

The writers chose to tell the movie in a flashback as a quasi detective story. It starts with Phil on the phone to Tracy, breaking the news to her that their bachelor party weekend "got a little out of control" and the wedding is "not going to happen." Then, we flashback to the series of bizarre events that got the characters to that point, coming full-circle to the phone call.

If writers Lucas and Moore had told it straight through from night to morning, it would have just been four drunks doing a series of dumb things. That story might have run out of steam by mid-second act, because seeing a drunk pull out his own tooth is not interesting as seeing an ugly gap in Stu's mouth and wondering why he is suddenly and mysteriously missing a front tooth.

This way, they built in mystery and rising tension along the way. And by leaving out key information, they make the information we do learned that much more compelling.

I suspect that early in their plotting process, the writers outlined the night chronologically as it truly progressed, then went back and said what would happen when the three main characters wake up and their memories of certain actions from the previous night are missing. And then other information comes back to them out of sequence. But notice how the clues they get do come in relative conformity to their chronological sequence from the night before. Otherwise, it might have been too confusing.

The writers also do a great job of letting character drive the plot. Phil is driven to correct his screw up, which is probably indicative of his marriage and life. Stu is compelled to save his friend, Doug, because Stu always puts others first. And Alan is compelled to go along for the adventure, because everything to him is fun and games.

Their individual characters drive their choices which, in turn, drive the plot.

Know Your Lead Character

Even in an ensemble piece like *The Hangover* or the *Anchorman* movies, it's important to know who your lead character is.

So, who is the lead character in *The Hangover*? It's an ensemble comedy, yes. But Phil (Bradley Cooper) is clearly the lead, because while Stu and Alan are *reactive*, Phil is *proactive*. It is not an accident that it's always Phil who is calling Tracy to say they screwed up and the wedding is off. Phil is the catalyst – the leader of the pack – who will either make the wedding happen or not. Stu and Alan could never have found Doug, even though Alan won the $82,000 they used to win Black Doug's freedom and Stu had the sudden realization that the word "roofies" leads to one to think of a roof, the place where Doug has been stuck all this time.

Without Phil, they never would have gone through the sequence of events that led them to "Black Doug" that led them to arguing about roofies and realizing Doug is on the hotel roof. Phil is the glue, the driving force, and the person who everyone relies on to make the story move forward.

Let's go through the same process with one of my all-time favorite comedy movies, *Anchorman: The Legend of Ron Burgundy*. The movie is essentially the story of Barbara Walters and Harry Reasoner, the first man-woman news anchor team on network television, a pairing that led to friction between them and disastrous ratings.

Here is the structure of *Anchorman*, as I break it down:

Anchorman: The Legend of Ron Burgundy

- **inciting incident** - the station hires a female reporter
- **plot point** - Ron convinces Veronica to go on a date
- **act break** - Veronica sees Ron as more than a work associate and they have sex
- **act two** - Ron and Veronica are now romantically involved

- **pinch point** - Ron's beloved dog Baxter is kicked into the river, making Ron late for the broadcast
- **midpoint** Voronica substitutes for Ron as anchor and is a hit. She is promoted toco-anchor, further damaging Ron's status and respect
- **rising tension** - Ron and Veronica break up
- **pinch-point** - Ron and guys try to sabotage Veronica, leading to their fistfight
- **rising tension** - Veronica and other women at the station decide to fight back
- **reversal** - Veronica's practical joke leads Ron to insult San Diego
- **act break** - Ron gets fired
- **act three** - Ron begins his descent into hell. He is abandoned by his peers and loses respect in the city he once ruled, then falls into drinking
- **pinch point** - a panda is giving birth at the San Diego Zoo and Veronica is sent to cover it
- **rising tension** - Veronica is pushed into bear cage by a competitor
- **reversal** - With Veronica missing, the station manager needs Ron to cover the Panda birth. Ron reunites with news team
- **climax** - Ron must choose between reporting the news and saving Veronica
- **resolution** - Baxter returns and saves Ron and Veronica. They make up and co-report the Panda birth, ultimately getting promoted to co-anchors of network news

The main plot is about Ron's career being threatened by a female co-anchor.

A subplot is Ron and Veronica's romance, with Ron falling in love for the first time.

Another subplot is Ron's escalating feud with his broadcasting rival, Wes Mantooth (Vince Vaughn). This particular subplot doesn't really drive the main plot all that much; it's mostly there for comedy and to fill out the required 90 minutes of screen time.

Notice that each act has a beginning, middle and end. Every 10-15 pages is a story point. About 8-10 in the script. And plot points are told in sequences, such as Veronica successfully anchoring the news, which leads to her and Ron breaking up.

Aside from the "F— you, San Diego" gag, you could probably write this story as a drama script and it would hold up.

Your Story

To beat out a movie story, we do it pretty much the same way we beat out a TV script. Every scene has 2-6 beats. Every 6-12 pages is a story point. And there are about 10-12 story points in the main plot of the script.

But, unlike a half-hour or one-hour TV script, a movie screenplay has a more elaborate act structure. Let's take a look at some of those elements.

ASSIGNMENT

COME UP WITH A MOVIE IDEA THAT YOU'D LIKE TO WRITE. THEN WATCH TWO MOVIES IN THAT PARTICULAR GENRE (ROMCOM, SILLY COMEDY, DRAMEDY, ETC.) AND READ TWO SCREENPLAYS FROM THAT GENRE.

22

FIRST ACTS

Laying the Foundation

As everyone knows, the first act introduces your lead characters, their goal (or desire) and the initial obstacle to achieving that goal. The first act can be fast paced and relentless, as in *Star Wars*, or it can be a more easy-going character study, as in *Rocky*.

By page ten or so, we should know what your movie is about and who it is about. That's a hard and fast rule of screenplay analysis. What readers call *the hook*. If you haven't introduced your lead (or two leads) and given us a vague notion of the conflict they are facing in the first ten minutes of your movie, you may start testing the patience of your audience (and script readers).

By page 25 or so, you should introduce a major plot point that will kick your story into high gear, set the stakes, and propel the characters into act two.

In *Rocky*, he learns he is going to fight for the heavyweight championship of the world.

In *The Hangover*, the guys wake up blacked out from the night before with no idea where the groom-to-be is.

In *The Holdovers*, Paul learns that he must spend Christmas break at school watching over the sad-sack students who have no place to go for the holidays.

Writing in Sequences

All successful screenplays can be broken down into *sequences* (a collection of scenes). In each sequence, the hero pursues some single, short-term goal. A sequence continues until our hero learns some fresh news that brings his/her pursuit of the current short-term goal to an end or creates a new goal. Sometimes, there can be two sequences happening simultaneously, as in *Anchorman*, where Ron is desperately running to get back to the station in time as Veronica successfully anchors her first solo newscast.

Make sure your Hero has a goal

A functional hero has a nemesis (which could be an antagonist, or could be another hero like his romantic partner, as in *When Harry Met Sally*). She/he has obstacles that get progressively harder. And we, as writers, keep throwing obstacles in his/her way until he's almost defeated, or appears defeated to the audience (as in *Rocky* when Rocky is down and seemingly out for the count).

In his book, The Story Solution, screenplay guru Eric Edson uses a term called *"the Hero Goal Sequence,"* in which the protagonist pursues a unique goal that seems out of his or her grasp. As Edson calculates it, act one has 6 hero goal sequences, culminating in a stunning surprise. The first half of act two has another 6 hero goal sequences. The movie's midpoint arrives at hero goal sequence #12. The second half of act two has 6 more hero goal sequences And the third act has 2-5 goal sequences.

I have never applied Edson's equation to an individual movie. But it's clear that his overall theory of movie structure makes sense, even if the number of sequences varies by film to film.

The first sequence of a movie locks the main character (or characters) into a quest that they cannot back out of. That's sometimes called "the lock-in." Now that the character is locked-in to her quest, she makes her first attempts to solve the problem. This is usually the simplest, easiest manner to resolve the problem, and these attempts usually fail.

It is important to show the *ramifications* of these attempts, which fail and often result in increasing complications. Every move the character makes traps them even more into their quest. Each action leads to deeper and deeper entrapment. Be merciless on the character by setting greater and greater traps that propel them forward.

Coincidence and Bad Luck

I mentioned when and when not to employ coincidences earlier in this book, but let's refresh our memory.

Coincidence and bad luck are okay if they work *against* your character, especially in the second half of act two. Virtually anything that works against your character now is acceptable. Any accident, any coincidence, any unfair result is fine because it makes his predicament worse.

We want our movie heroes to have *worse luck* than us. But not better luck, because that feels artificial and contrived.

Obstacles

The second act is all about obstacles. It elaborates in great detail and intensity on the difficulties and setbacks the hero faces as they struggle to achieve their goal.

Just when we think the situation can't get worse, it does. And when there is no way that our hero can get out of the jam, they do get out, only to end up in a *worse jam*.

Let's look at the classic comedy movie, *Airplane!* When people think about *Airplane!*, they generally don't think it had much of a plot. But it actually did.

In the first act, flight attendant Elaine breaks off her romantic relationship with Ted Striker. That is the inciting incident. Now Ted has a problem: he has to win Elaine back. So, he buys a ticket for the flight she's leaving on. But on the plane, she refuses to talk to him. That leads to Ted's second obstacle, we learn that he's terrified of air travel ("ever since the war") and he begins to suffer his "drinking problem" again. When the captain and his flight crew suddenly become incapacitated, Ted faces his third problem: he has to fly and land the massive jumbo jet, a plane he's never flown before. Which eventually leads to his fourth and fifth problems: the weather is particularly terrorizing that night, and the man in air traffic control who is going to help guide the plane to the ground is a former military associated of Ted's that he hates. Each of these "beats" is really a sequence of scenes that explain the plot points.

Each *sequence* centers around a new obstacle or obstacles of increasing difficulty, upping the stakes and often making the problem worse.

The end of the first act is *"the lock-in,"* locking the hero into a problem and obstacle (winning Elaine back) that he will have to overcome before their life can get back to some semblance of normal.

ASSIGNMENT

COME UP WITH 50 CARDS FOR SCENES, JOKES, OR SEQUENCES IN YOUR MOVIE. READ TWO MORE SCREENPLAYS, THIS TIME DRAMAS. THINK ABOUT HOW YOU WOULD TELL THAT SAME STORY AS A COMEDY.

23

SECOND ACTS

Moving from Lock-in to Fixes

The second act begins right after the lock-in: the moment when the character is stuck in the predicament and main tension. (Ted is trapped on a plane that has no flight crew.) It's too late to turn back (they're in the air), so they must go forward (find a new pilot).

Now the main character aims towards his revised goal (land safely and win back Elaine) and has the first run-in with his obstacles (landing a plane he's never flown) and antagonists (Rex Kramer, Ted's former commanding officer who Ted hates and who has no confidence in Ted's ability to fly).

Each *fix* creates a new set of obstacles, always crafted by the writers with *rising actions* and *rising tension.*

It's true, the plot of *Airplane!* is somewhat goofy and unbelievable. Yet the structure of the story holds up, and could even be the makings of a drama film if the tone of the dialogue was less surreal. Indeed, *Airplane!* was a parody of several real life drama movies that were popular at that time. And the plots of those melodramatic films weren't far off from the satiric version.

How to Conquer Your Second Act

The first rule is, know your character's goal and stay clearly focused on it. Much of the second act will be dedicated to his/her pursuit of this goal. So, unless your main character has a clearly defined goal, you will always struggle with your second act.

Without a goal propelling her (and the plot) forward, what you may end up left with is a serialized, sketch-like, rambling second act.

Of course, there are some exceptions to this rule (just like there are exceptions to everything in life), such as *The Way, Way Back* and *Lost In Translation*. But even there, the sequences are propelled by a want that the lead character has. In *The Way, Way Back,* fourteen year old Duncan wants a normal family. In *Lost in Translation*, fading American celebrity Bob Harris (Bill Murray) wants to find love and meaning in his life. In both films, the writers take us through a series of sequences that build on those wants.

The Midpoint Whack

The second act is the longest act in your movie, and if you don't structure it properly, it might end up meandering and losing focus. So screenwriters use the *midpoint* (about 60 pages into the script) to add a major story twist, re-focus the lead character on her/his quest, up the stakes, and re-grab the audience.

Think of it as a 2x4 to the audience's head. They're getting lulled into a predictable story pattern, so you *whack them* with a major change in direction. It could be a twist, reversal or major escalation of the stakes. It could be the main character coming to a different, more profound understanding of the challenge they are facing. Whatever you choose, it should jumpstart the second half of your movie and grab the audience all over again.

In the Oscar-winning screenplay, *Rain Man* (written by Barry Morrow and Ronald Bass), that might be the moment where

Charlie Babbitt (Tom Cruise) realizes that his autistic brother, Raymond (Dustin Hoffman), was the imaginary "rain man" Charlie vaguely remembers from his childhood who once saved infant Charlie from scalding hot bath water. Now, Charlie realizes that he's not only a caretaker for his older, autistic brother, but his brother was once a caretaker for him, bonding cold-hearted Charlie closer to Raymond.

The Fall

The end of your second act is when your character has overcome some or all the previous obstacles. He's managed to change a bit while keeping his relationships together. (Or, maybe they've fallen totally apart.) He may even believe he's overcome his fatal flaw.

But then, everything starts to crumble down on top of him. He loses the girl. He fails to vanquish the villain. He falls back into his own ways and bad habits. His fatal flaw seems magnified and insurmountable.

In *The Hangover*, Phil and Stu's fatal flaw is that they are both dumber than they realize. So they hand over $82,000 to Chow only to buy the freedom of the wrong "Doug." It hadn't occurred to them to confirm who the bag-head hostage was before making the exchange. And even though it's a giant coincidence that the man they bought has the same first name as their missing friend, we accept that coincidence because it works against them.

Now, they are broke again with a banged up Mercedes Benz and one less front tooth, still have no idea where the real Doug is, and are almost out of time to find him and get him back for the wedding. Everything seems lost. It's time for Phil to call Tracy and break the bad news to her.

In *Rocky*, the second act ends when he returns home from the massive boxing arena and tells Adrian that he can't win. His fatal flaw is his own insecurity and lack of self-respect, and it's now back in full force. Adrian, being the supportive partner that she is, doesn't argue the point. Maybe on some level she knew that all along. So, she simply asks him, "What are we going to do?"

But, in a brilliant writing twist, the screenwriter (Sylvester Stallone) uses that moment to change Rocky's goal. He says he no longer has to win. He tells her that no one has ever "gone the distance" with Apollo Creed, so if he can just do that, he'll feel like a winner.

The last 10-15 pages of your second act illustrates the steady decline of your main character, ending with him at the lowest point of his life.

Phil having to tell Tracy he lost her fiancée and the wedding is off.

Kristin Wiig losing her boyfriend and best friend in *Bridesmaids*.

Rocky realizing he can't beat Apollo Creed.

The end of your second act should look like it's over for you character. That there's no hope. And with that, you've concluded your second act and are ready to leap into the third.

Weave in Subplots

No story can be about just one problem or relationship. You need a solid sub-plot (or subplots) that carefully intertwines with the main tension in both tone and theme.

Your subplot will is a vehicle in which to relate the lead character's emotions in regard to the main tension.

In *The Hangover*, a subplot is Stu's terrible relationship with his own fiancée. Stu wants to save Doug's marriage by saving Doug. But his own horrible relationship makes him question the institution of marriage and his understanding of love. Is a marriage really worth saving? For Stu, the answer ends up being mixed: 'yes' for saving Doug's wedding day, but 'no' for continuing in his own poisonous courtship.

The Third Act: Barreling to the Finish Line

Third acts are the easiest to conceive and the hardest to pull off. That's because you have a lot of tasks to complete. You have to drive toward a surprising, satisfying resolution. You have to resolve unresolved relationships. And you have to tie up the loose ends of your subplots. (Often times, those last two elements are one and the same.)

Plus, you need to devise an ending that makes sense from the view of where the story began. That often requires foreshadowing. But what if you come up with a great idea for a boffo ending that you didn't know was coming as you were writing your rough draft?

Simple: go back and plant the seeds in the early scenes. Maybe that's just a line of dialogue or a visual you go back and drop in somewhere along the way. Or maybe it will require a brand new scene or sequence. Don't be afraid to go back and reinvent the wheel of your first or second act. Oftentimes, that's how the best foreshadowing is created – after the fact.

Final Shots

Your movie's closing sequence and final shot are often the emotional button on the story, a way of transitioning us out of the fictional narrative into a place of understanding and acceptance. Quite often, its a pullback or an overhead shot that pulls out from the intimacy of a moment: your characters riding a two-person bike together, driving off into the distance, or in a western, riding off into the sunset. Other times, it might be abrupt, like a sudden cut to black or a close-up on a key detail in the scene that we didn't quite notice before. In a murder mystery, maybe a key piece of evidence that the detectives never found.

You will spend hours and days trying to perfect this final moment of your script, because you want to "wow" the reader and leave them emotionally spent.

But, guess what: your great finale idea will never been seen on screen. Directors usually come up with their own idea for a final shot – often employing some visual camera trick they've been dying to use on their last three projects.

To put it metaphorically, you've just spent days designing the perfect casket to lay your beloved characters to rest, and the director decides on cremation.

So, don't spend too much time "directing" your screenplay. Lay out the story and the scenes and let a director figure out how to bring that story to life on screen.

Assignment

Lay out your major plot points in a visual script paradigm like the one below.

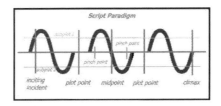

Once you're happy with the paradigm, start writing your movie, using the same system I taught in the TV writing chapters. Go from beat sheet to treatment (outline), and then begin to morph your treatment into formatted script scenes.

24

FILM CHARACTERS

The overarching purpose of the second act of your screenplay is to explore your characters. Sure, the plot has to move forward. But your plot is just a device to allow you (and your audience) to learn about your characters and see how they handle life.

All of this starts with your lead character's defining flaw – or "fatal flaw" – the thing that's held your character back his/her entire life. Once you identify that flaw, the plot is a journey you create to test that flaw over and over. Quite often, the fatal flaw is insecurity, feeling unloved, or narcissism.

In *Saving Private Ryan* (by Robert Rodat), the fatal flaw was cowardice. (Or, more accurately, what Tom Hank's Captain Miller character perceived as his own cowardice). (Though we come to learn that Capt. Miller was not really a coward; he was just an ordinary man caught in the extraordinary hell of war.) Miller confronted and tested his fatal flaw in combat, always somehow surviving to his unending amazement.

In *The Matrix* (by Lana and Lilly Wachowski), Neo's fatal flaw is that he doesn't believe in himself. Therefore, many of the scenes in the second act test that problem. The building jump.

The dojo fight. The Oracle visit. The subway fight. Each time, that lack of belief is being tested. And each time, he comes a little closer to believing in himself.

In *Rocky*, his fatal flaw is his own insecurity and lack of self-esteem. The world has beaten those self-doubts into him, and in his quest to prepare for the title fight (the second act), he must not only reshape his body, he must reshape his own self-respect.

In *The Holdovers*, we initially think that the goal of teacher Paul Hunham (Paul Giamatti) is to educate his students so they may progress in life, and his obstacle is that they are all pampered, spoiled and unmotivated. But, by mid-movie, we learn that his true obstacle in life is his own self-doubt and inability to break out of the rut of his miserable existence. He says, "I find the world a bitter and complicated place, and it seems to feel the same way about me."

The twist of the movie is that he ultimately learns from his problematic student, Angus, that rebelling and occasionally saying 'screw you' to the world is the true path to personal progress and self-redemption.

His *test* is standing up to Angus's uncaring parents. It costs him his job, but he finds self-redemption in finally being able to stand up to the bitter disappointments of his life and move on. Notice that the movie begins with him handing out test results and assigning his students a new test immediately after Christmas break. But the movie's plot is really a test he must take for himself. A test he ultimately passes by failing (much like his history class.)

He may have failed his Christmas Break assignment in the eyes of the school headmaster who fires him. But he progresses in life by learning to really care about a student (Angus), act on that caring by doing what's best in Angus's behalf, and thereby break the invisible chains that have been tying him down at the school for decades.

These tests force your characters to grow, which will in turn bring us closer to the character and find us rooting for him.

By the way, here's a test for you: is *The Holdovers* a comedy or a drama?

The answer: It doesn't matter. It's a movie that holds together no matter how you receive it, as a light holiday comedy or as a serious life lesson. And that's the best kind of movie to write.

Character Change

Throughout the second act, the main character starts changing, learning, adapting, and developing. Or, intense pressure is put on the character to change and that change will manifest in character growth in the third act. This pressure to change, initially resisted by the character, ultimately forces the character to understand themselves better and come up with a different response to old problems. They develop a new back-bone (so to speak), determination, ingenuity, bravery, fearlessness, and resolve.

Sometimes, what drives the second act plot is the character's *resistance to change*. In *The Holdovers*, prep school teacher Paul Hunham is a rigid, curmudgeonly ass at the top of the film and seems immune to any outward showing of human emotion well into the second act. It's only at the midpoint, when we see him confronted with his past and his failures in life, that he lets down his guard and starts to show a vulnerable side to Angus and to us.

Secondary Character Flaws

It doesn't necessarily have to be your hero who has the flaw. Many times it's a secondary character who does the changing in a story.

In *Star Wars* (by George Lucas), Han Solo's flaw is that he's a narcissist. That flaw is tested when he and Luke Skywalker get into arguments over strategy, when he's given the chance to save the princess, and when he's given a chance to join the Death Star battle. (Notice the tests build.)

In *Ferris Bueller's Day Off* (by John Hughes), Cameron's flaw is that he doesn't take chances in life.

Virtually every scene in the movie is Cameron being given a chance to let loose, to "enjoy life." From driving his dad's car to the French restaurant to the baseball game to the parade. But it is Ferris who drives Cameron's goal. Our hero is forcing the change in the secondary character.

Resolve Relationships

Relationships are the other main way you're going to explore your characters in your second act.

You'd like to establish two or three unresolved relationships in your movie, and you want to use your second act to begin to resolve them.

In *Annie Hall* (by Woody Allen and Marshall Brickman), those are Alvy's relationship with his ex-wife, Allison Portchnik (Carole Kane), his relationship with Annie (Diane Keaton), and his relationship with his best friend, Rob (Tony Roberts).

There's usually a key issue in every relationship that needs to be fixed. Many of the scenes and sequences in your second act will be used to explore those issues.

In *Good Will Hunting* (by Matt Damon and Ben Affleck), the three biggest relationships are Will and Sean (Robin Williams), Will and Skylar (Minnie Driver), and Will and Professor Lambeau (Stellan Skarsgård).

The key issue with Will and Sean is Will being unable to open up.

The key issue with Will and Skylar is fear of commitment.

The key issue with Will and Professor Lambeau is what to do with Will's mathematical talent.

In *Rocky*, Rocky Balboa has all sorts of contentious relationships he needs to fix. In the second act, he needs to resolve his relationships with the painfully shy girl he likes, Adrian, her domineering brother, Paulie, and his disapproving manager, Mick. In the third act, he resolves his relationship with Apollo Creed (through their boxing match) and, by going the distance and proving to the world he has worth, he resolves his relationship with himself.

Each relationship needs to be resolved in some form or fashion for the movie to succeed. Even if that "resolution" is a painful breakup of a marriage, as in the ending in *Ordinary People*.

In *When Harry Met Sally* (by Nora Ephron), their unresolved issue is trying to remain friends. When they first meet, they don't really like each other so it doesn't matter. They are content to be frenemies and settle into an unspoken pact to live separate lives. But then they re-meet and start spending more time around each other, making that pact more difficult to abide.

Then they start dating other people while still confining in each other, making it yet more difficult.

Then they start a romantic relationship with each other, making it *even more* difficult.

So the act of trying to remain frenemies becomes more and more challenging by building in obstacles in front of that goal. The enemies-to-lovers trope has been around since the early years of film. Harry and Sally took it to a whole new level.

ASSIGNMENT

CONTINUE WRITING YOUR SCREENPLAY. AS AN EXERCISE, LIST TWO FATAL FLAWS AND TWO UNRESOLVED RELATIONSHIPS FOR EACH OF YOUR MAIN CHARACTERS AND MAJOR SECONDARY CHARACTERS.

25

THIRD ACTS

Third acts are the easiest to conceive and the hardest to pull off. That's because you have a lot of tasks to complete. You have to drive toward a surprising, satisfying resolution. You have to resolve unresolved relationships. And you have to tie up the loose ends of your subplots. (Often times, those last two elements are one and the same.)

Plus, you need to devise an ending that makes sense from the view of where the story began. That often requires foreshadowing. But what if you come up with a great idea for a boffo ending that you didn't know was coming as you were writing your rough draft?

Simple: go back and plant the seeds in the early scenes. Maybe that's just a line of dialogue or a visual you go back and drop in somewhere along the way. Or maybe it will require a brand new scene or sequence. Don't be afraid to go back and reinvent the wheel of your first or second act. Oftentimes, that's how the best foreshadowing is created – after the fact.

Final Shots

Your movie's closing sequence and final shot are often the emotional button on the story, a way of transitioning us out of the fictional narrative into a place of understanding and acceptance. Quite often, its a pullback or an overhead shot that pulls out from the intimacy of a moment: your characters riding a two-person bike together, driving off into the distance, or in a western, riding off into the sunset. Other times, it might be abrupt, like a sudden cut to black or a close-up on a key detail in the scene that we didn't quite notice before. In a murder mystery, maybe a key piece of evidence that the detectives never found.

You will spend hours and days trying to perfect this final moment of your script, because you want to "wow" the reader and leave them emotionally spent.

But, guess what: your great finale idea will never been seen on screen. Directors usually come up with their own idea for a final shot – often employing some visual camera trick they've been dying to use on their last three projects.

To put it metaphorically, you've just spent days designing the perfect casket to lay your beloved characters to rest, and the director decides on cremation.

So, don't spend too much time "directing" your screenplay. Lay out the story and the scenes and let a director figure out how to bring that story to life on screen.

Lessons From the Trenches

Development Hell is an industry term for the period of time immediately after you've optioned or sold your screenplay. Now, everyone from the studio executives and their minions to the agents, director, actors (if any are attached), the legal department, the marketing departments, and a slew of other players are giving you notes and forcing you to make changes to this perfect child of a script that you birthed into this world on your own.

It will change in development, in casting, in pre-production, in rewrites for cast and locations, in more pre-production, on the set, in editing, and probably in twenty steps I haven't named. And each time, your heart will break just a little bit more.

That's why it's called "hell." You should be so lucky to get there. Because you can't get from screenplay to finished movie without it.

I had one movie project where the producers loved my script right up until the point where the production company head said he didn't understand the second act. He'd already optioned the script and intended to produce it, but he didn't understand two-thirds of the story.

Right there, in the middle of the meeting, one junior producer who had been telling me what a creative genius I was for weeks and months as I turned in sequence after sequence, flipped on a dime by saying, "Yeah, I never understood why Kevin did that, either."

As you might expect, that led to more rewrites and more drafts until the "genius" of the original story got lost in a deadly crossfire of half-baked notes and wayward creative impulses. The movie never got made. At least, not my version.

A few years later, I saw a trailer for a new movie coming out with the same title, featuring the same basic premise, produced by the same studio. Coincidence? Hmm. Even though my script was a comedy and the finished film was clearly a drama starring two huge A-list dramatic actors, I got curious and shelled out a few bucks to see it on opening day.

Not only did the film have my title, but their movie and my script shared a lot of similar plot points. Okay, that can happen, I thought. Once you have the basic premise, the major plot points lay out fairly obviously.

But the thing that really made me skeptical was the name of the lead character. In my script, he was a young, hotshot attorney named Spencer Lomax. A fairly original, unusual name, I felt. Yet the lead character in the movie version was also a young, hotshot attorney with an uncannily similar name name, Kevin Lomax.

At home, I wondered how they end up with that name in the movie they produced. My best guess was, some junior development executive at the studio had my script in front of her during a pre-production meeting. In my imagination, a studio bigwig said he didn't like the last name of the young attorney in their script and asked for suggestions. So the development exec looks at my script, sees the last name of my lead character, and pitches, "Hey, what about 'Lomax'?" Bigwig: "Lomax? 'Kevin Lomax.' Yeah, sure, that'll work." Again, this is just a fantasy scenario I dreamed up. I have no hard evidence that my script was purloined.

Was I angry or bitter? No. The drama movie was far enough off from my comedy screenplay that I figured it's more of a compliment than an insult. I got paid for my work, and my script was never going to be made at that studio either way. They used my comedy script as source material to produce a suspense-horror drama and it turned out pretty good. I took that as a pat on the back and moved on with my career.

Read, Read, Read

My final tip to anyone who wants to write a screenplay is to read them. As many as you can. Comedies, dramas, box office hits, little army movies, scripts that got purchased for zillions of bucks, blacklist scripts of potentially great films that never got made.

When I was learning the craft, you had to scrounge scripts from your agent, trade them with writer friends, or buy them at brick-and-mortar script stores that sold copies of produced screenplays for $15 bucks each. (Imagine all the intellectual property violations they were racking up!)

Today, you can simple Google a movie title and the term

".pdf" and chances are you'll find the script you want online. It may be a shooting script or a very early draft that bears little resemblance to the final film. They both have value.

I love to read early drafts of movies I love to see how much the script changed over time.

In an early draft of *Anchorman*, the movie took place in Portland (not San Diego), the zoo was expecting the birth of a baby giraffe (not a panda), and the third act was about Alicia being kidnapped by a 1970s-style ultra-radical political group and Ron having to save her.

In the movie *Rocky*, he learns that he's going to fight Apollo for the title about 23 minutes into the movie, the end of the first act. In an early draft I read, it's the midpoint of the screenplay, with a lot more first and second act padding about Rocky's job as a collector for a loan shark and his attempts to woo Adrian. I've heard that the original draft Stallone wrote and showed to his friends, Rocky was a cruel, violent street thug and there wasn't even a girlfriend character.

And in the earliest versions of *The Hangover*...

• Phil (Bradley Cooper) is named "Vick" and is an unmarried, shyster businessman (not a teacher)

• Stu and Alan's names are flipped

• Alan (later Stu, played by Ed Helms) is an accountant (not a dentist) who wakes up from their hangover with an embarrassing mullet instead of a missing tooth

• Stu (later Alan, played by Zach Galifianakis) is a married father of two kids and manager of an Applebees (not the dimwitted unemployed brother of the bride-to-be)

• Jade (Heather Graham) was named Chastity

• Leslie Chow (played by the diminutive Ken Jeong) is an immensely large man named Jimmy Lang who was a former business associate of Vick's

• there was no abandoned baby or tiger in their suite, no Mike

Tyson sequence, no mention of Stu (Alan) being a Black Jack savant, no reference to "roofies"...

Well, you get the idea. Although the basic structure was the same, it was a very different script. Still hysterical, but not the *Hangover* movie we came to know and love.

The moral of this chapter: don't be afraid to dream up a movie comedy and put it on paper...or a laptop screen, or whatever method you use to write. And don't think it has to be perfect (though you'll try to make it as perfect as you can). It only has to be funny and make sense.

The rest is a combination of luck, talent, connections, persistence, and more luck. Many great screenplays have never been made and many lousy ones have.

May yours be great *and* be made!

FADE OUT.

ASSIGNMENT

FINISH YOUR SCREENPLAY. REWRITE IT. GET NOTES. REWRITE IT AGAIN. GET MORE NOTES. MAKE IT AS PERFECT AS YOU CAN. SELL IT TO A PRODUCER OR MOVIE STUDIO. MENTION ME IN YOUR OSCAR SPEECH.

THE BUSINESS OF HOLLYWOOD

THE BUSINESS OF
HOLLYWOOD

26

THE TV MARKETPLACE

Your industry Calling Card

The spec script is the writer's calling card to the industry. It is 80% of what it takes to land a TV writing job. (The other 20% is how well you interview and how funny you are in person.) So, do you need to have a great one? No. You need 2-3 great ones.

Even if an agent or network executive reads and likes one of your scripts, they are going to ask, "What else ya got?" So be ready. Most writers spec out two different types of shows within their target genre. In the case of half-hours, you should have one "hip" show (such as *Modern Family*, an NBC Thursday night show, or an HBO/Showtime/cable show such as *Veep, Girls, Nurse Jackie, or Louie*) and one of the less hip shows (maybe even a Disney or Nickelodeon series). That way, no matter what type of series an agent wants to submit you for, you have a writing sample within that sub-genre.

Once you have one of each, write more. Never stop writing specs. The *Modern Family* you just finished will probably not be as good as the *Girls* spec you write next. Even if your current spec is

top tier, it will also be one-year older next hiring season and you'll
want to give your agent new ammo to help market you.

So, keep churning them out. I knew one very successful
sitcom producer who had to write thirty-five specs before he
landed his first job. Even when I was a supervising producer of
network series, I always wrote a new spec every season (usually
for a series I wanted to work for). And even though I had been
writing for years, my specs still got better over time. Yours
will, too.

The Staff Job

Okay, so you wrote a great spec script (or two, or twelve) and
you somehow got it to someone who showed it to somebody, who
gave it to a very important somebody, who told an even more
important somebody, about you and that somebody read it,
brought you in for a meeting, and hired you on the staff of their
show. (Usually there's many more "somebodies" in the middle but
I used the streamlined version.)

You show up on day one, having spent the last year or two
writing spec scripts in the solitude of your
home/office/dorm/Starbucks. Now you're in a room with 6-10
other writers, and you are expected to "write" with them...out
loud...without your keyboard and under the pressure to "be funny
for money." What do you do?

The first thing is, listen! Figure out who the power people are
in the room, the person, or people you need to please to get your
lines into the show. Then, see how they talk and who they listen
to. Hear the rhythm of the room. Don't be too serious but don't
laugh too hard. At first their chatter will probably be whizzing by
you like heavy flak in a firefight. You'll be overwhelmed. Don't
panic. It's normal.

When you think of a line, try to jot down a couple of key

words before you pitch it. In a fast room you may not have time. Regardless, don't worry if it's not perfect. Try to get the essence of the line out. If it's funny, someone will build on it or maybe reword it, so it pops.

(However, be careful not to become the person who is constantly rewording other people's lines. You need to pitch original stuff, not just build on everyone else's ideas.)

On some shows, I hit the ground running the first day. On others, it took me two days to get into the groove. Producers will usually be understanding in your first week or so. The trick is to get into the rhythm of the other writers, figure out who scores the most, and emulate them.

When you know what script you'll be working on for a given day, you want to spend several hours with it before the meeting. Look for weak jokes that you can replace with better ones and jot yours down. Sometimes have 2-3 alternatives for a line you think can be beaten. Word them out exactly and practice saying them out loud. Then practice them again! Once in the room, try not to let on that you are reading prepared lines. Make it seem like you're coming up with them on the spot. Lines that seem spontaneous get the biggest laughs.

And don't pitch against a line that got a laugh yesterday unless you are darn sure that yours is better.

The most important thing to remember is, be positive. Don't knock a line unless you have an alternative. The rule is, beat it or leave it. Producers love someone who can make the room laugh and add to a script. Conversely, they can't stand staffers who tear down material but never bring anything to the table.

Partnering & Collaborating

If you're like most readers, you will be writing your script by yourself. But you may be feeling pretty lonely right about this point in the process and wishing you had a partner to lean on. That's not always a bad instinct. Partners can make life easier – especially in comedy writing.

So, if you're looking around wondering where to find a writing partner, look no further than your local writing classes. They are the perfect place to network, trade ideas, see who shares your comedic sensibilities, and make the connection. Even if you live in separate cities (or countries), a partnership is feasible if you don't mind distance collaborating and are both willing to relocate to LA or NY if you landed a TV staff job.

How would that work, you ask? Actually, not much differently than a lot of teams work today. Many teams talk out a story in a single meeting (which you could do on Zoom) and then each partner takes an act and runs with it. Then they trade, make notes and proposed changes on each other's scenes, put it together and do a polish pass to fix any remaining inconsistencies. (which, you could also do through emails or by phone/Skype).

Is it as easy as living in the same town? Maybe not, but there's a lot less commuting and you have the added benefit of two very different life views to draw on. So, it's worth thinking about.

You can also look for partners in your local area, in on-sight writing classes, or writers' groups. Or just put out feelers on Facebook and Instagram (or whatever is the new, hot site that I haven't learned about yet). Sure, these are long shots, but if you want to break into big-time comedy writing, you'll need to explore and exploit every single avenue.

Once you find a potential partner, talk at length about the types of shows and comedy you like, how you write, and what your career goals are. Do a one-time test script together to see how well you collaborate. Make it clear that you'll both own the end product, and neither will market it without the other's name on it. And keep a paper trail (or email trail) of all your shared work.

And don't get too disillusioned if your first collaboration doesn't go absolutely perfectly. Just like anything else, team writing is a learned skill. It takes time to get it right.

Why partner? There's a school of thought that a team of writers is more salable than a solo because a show is getting two writers for the price of one. (Yes, if you didn't know, writing teams share a salary...unless they are in high demand.) And if you happen to be of different sexes or races – or both! – so much the better. (One team of writers - one Chinese and one Latino - became known in the TV community as "Rice and Beans"and they never stopped working. No lie.)

Finding a partner is like finding a spouse. You need to have different strengths but see the world through one lens. Most teams I've met have one partner who's better at story and one who's better at punch-up.One who likes to drive the keyboard and one who prefers to write out loud. That's not a rule, but it's been my observation.

Just remember, as important as it is to choose someone who thinks like you and is really talented, you also have to find someone whom you trust to represent your career. There's nothing worse than being at the mercy of a partner who other people dislike. You may get a staff job together off the strength of your scripts, but the damage a jerky partner can do to their own reputation will stick to your reputation as well. So, choose wisely.

ASSIGNMENT

OF COURSE, ALL THESE "ASSIGNMENTS" ARE JUST SUGGESTIONS. THIS WEEK I SUGGEST YOU BREAK OUT OF THE TELEVISION MINDSET FOR A FEW HOURS AND READ ONE OR TWO GREAT SCREENPLAYS. SEE WHAT MAKES THEM DIFFERENT FROM TV SCRIPTS. WHICH STYLE DO YOU PREFER? IF YOU ARE UP TO THE CHALLENGE, START THINKING ABOUT A MOVIE IDEA YOU MIGHT LIKE TO WRITE. IF YOU WANT TO BREAK INTO THE BUSINESS, IT HELPS TO BE MULTIFACETED IN WHAT FORMS AND

GENRES YOU CAN WRITE. HAVING A SPEC SCREENPLAY (OR STAGE PLAY) TO GO ALONG WITH YOUR PILOT AND HALF-HOUR SPEC WILL MAKE YOU THAT MUCH MORE ATTRACTIVE TO AN AGENT (ONCE YOU CAN GET ONE TO SPEAK TO YOU).

27

CHARTING YOUR CAREER

You may think it's premature to talk about a TV writing career after a few lessons in a book. And for most of you, it may be.

But every year a couple of my UCLA Extension Writers' Program students break into the business, and in almost every class I've taught I saw at least one student whom I thought could do it. I took two UCLA Extension writing courses when I was starting out, and people I took those classes with went on to have very successful careers as well.

So why not you?

Your Next Script

As I said at the end of the last chapter, you should already be thinking about your next spec script. If it's for TV, hopefully you know what show you want to write and even have a germ of an idea.

If you don't, start now. Pick a different show than the one you just wrote. It's usually advisable to try a different sub-genre. So, if you wrote a family-based series *The Garcias,* try a workplace series like *Ted Lasso or Hacks,* or a broad comedy show like *Young Sheldon* or *Young Rock.* (Or take a classic show and create your own "*Young_____*" spec pilot.) Push your boundaries.

You may be thinking, *I'm a COMEDY writer! I watch SNL, loved Arrested Development, and hope to create the next Schitt's Creek someday. Why in the world would I write a Young Sheldon"spec?!*

The answer is: because those may be the types of shows you have a shot at. Sorry to break the news to you, but as hard as it is to break into TV writing, it's even harder to break in on a stellar, cutting-edge show that every great writer in LA and NY wants to work on.

Look at it this way: if you were single and hoping to find a husband or wife, would you limit your market to only the handsomest, hottest in-demand celebrities? Because that's what those shows are. So, if you want to hold out for a perfect ten, be my guest. But your new agent may not be willing to hold out for just those shows. And you may not get offered one for your first or second gig.

Agents who sign new writers expect them to go up for every job opening, and that includes the kiddie shows and soft network sitcoms that you may not necessarily watch for pleasure. If you tell your new CAA agent you don't want to be put up for those shows, she may say okay and be polite about it. But there's a decent chance they'll get frustrated and stop submitting you for anything pretty soon. What salesman wants to represent someone who would turn down work?

So, even if you think of yourself as an artist or comedic genius, be ready to take meetings for shows you don't like. Once you're hired on one, you'll learn to like it or tolerate it.

Chuck Lorre (creator of *The Big Bang Theory* and *Two and a Half Men*) once wrote for *Charles in Charge, Beany and Cecil,* and *Muppet Babies.* Jenji Kohan (*Weeds, Orange Is the New Black*) started on *Fresh Prince of Bel Air.* If they can start like that, so can you.

But you'll need to have at least two – and probably three or four – really tight, really solid scripts to show before you'll be able to get an agent or a full-time writing job. That's because most smart producers (and they're all smart these days) will want to read you a few times before entrusting you with a freelance assignment or a staff position.

One great script isn't going to cut it.

The other reason to jump into a new script is it will give you time and perspective on the old one. That just-finished *Always Sunny in Philadelphia* spec you think is so perfect may seem a lot less perfect in a month's time when you're not as close to it.

And every script you write will make you a smarter, stronger writer.

I wrote eleven spec half-hour scripts before I got my first sitcom staff job. I know good writers who wrote more than thirty. You are never done writing specs until you are a showrunner, and even then, you may decide to write something on spec to jump-start your career.

Sometimes writers on less-than-stellar series will write a spec to prove they have the chops to work on the A-list shows. TV history is replete with stories of working writer-producers on mediocre shows who used their hiatus to spec a great show, and then got a better job on a terrific show thanks to that new sample script. (Even the executive producers of *The Jeffersons* famously wrote a spec *Cheers* to move up to that class of writing.)

So, write, and write, and write. Then, write some more.

Getting an Agent

Ah, the age-old question: how do I get an agent?

Let's just say you have to do a lot of research, network with a lot of people, and keep getting your work out there. It's that simple. And that hard.

Any agent is better than none; just don't sign a multi-year

contract unless you are darn sure they really have the connections and the reputation necessary to get people work. Some agents talk a good game, but they just want to sign you so if YOU get yourself a job, they get 10%.

Some are arm-chair writers who will have you do endless rewrites on your stuff until THEY are happy with it, then they'll send it out to one or two people and if it doesn't generate a job offer immediately, they'll never submit it again. And that's *after* you've done countless rewrites to please them.

Some are playing an angle that you can't see.

Some are just shysters.

But many are also good salesmen who just want a fresh face to rep, and they will work their tails off for you. They may not be big yet, but they will be someday. And if you are fortunate enough to get signed by that person at the early part of their rise, it could pay off handsomely. I hate to admit it, but I left a few young agents too soon, only to see them become major players while I languished at my new agency I'd left them for.

Okay, you want to hear my agent "horror story?" Here goes, but no names. Some of these people are still friends of mine.

In the 1990s, I felt I had plateaued in my career and was restless to get on one of the hotter shows of the time. I had been with my current agent for eight years, but I felt he was not bringing me the A-list offers I desired. Then, at a comedy festival in Aspen, I happened to run into the absolute hottest young agent in the business. I don't mean A top agent; I mean THE top agent — the one at the hottest agency who repped the most in-demand young talent. I had known him when he was a junior agent at my agency, before he leap-frogged to the new agency and took Hollywood by storm!

At the party, we make small talk for a few moments with our significant others, then he says I should call him when we're both "back in town."

I could barely contain my excitement. A few days after the festival ended, I called his office and set up the meeting. Sure enough, at that pow-wow he offered to sign me, and introduced me to another agent, a woman, who would be helping to represent me at the agency. With two powerhouse agents asking me to sign with them, it wasn't even a close call. I was sure I was just a signature away from working on *Frasier* or *Seinfeld*. So, I broke the news to my longtime agent and said my goodbyes. (He never spoke to me again.)

Two weeks later, I get a call from a very young, junior agent at the agency. She said, "I'm sure you heard the news. But don't worry, I am going to be your new agent here."

Whaaaat???

"What news?" I ask. She explained to me that that hotter-than-hot male agent who had just signed me had been let go after some allegations of sexual harassment by him toward another agent in the company.

"Oh, wow," I stammered. But that was only one of my two signing agents. "What about _____?" I asked her.

"Ohh." (PAINFULLY LONG PAUSE ON HER END) "She was the person who claimed he sexually harassed her. And she has decided to leave the agency as well."

My jaw dropped. How could both my agents be bolting the agency just fourteen days after I had signed with them?!

"But again, don't worry," said the newly-minted agent, a woman in her mid-twenties who had just been promoted out of the mailroom. "You have been assigned to me. And I'm thrilled to be working with you. But if you don't hear back from me for a while, don't worry about it. The whole agency is in turmoil with this change, and it will take a few weeks to sort everything out."

Which I knew meant a few months while the agency was mired in sexual harassment lawsuit depositions.

Now, this was just weeks before a new hiring season, so I

didn't have much choice. I hung in there and she did indeed place me on a new show for the next season. But it was not the kind of A-list show I wanted to work on, or anything close. And it was cancelled in a few short months.

During that time, the young mailroom émigré who was my new lead agent seemed overwhelmed in the role and not that sharp. Even though my new show's star had a development deal with the studio and wanted to develop one of my pilot ideas, she was unable to parlay that into an overall deal for me.

After a few more months of rarely returned calls and seeming ineffectiveness, I dropped her and changed agencies once again.

The upshot: things didn't get better with the new, new agency. And that young, untested agent went on to become one of the hottest agents in the business in her own right. And then the president of a major cable network. And then one of Forbes' Top 20 Most Powerful Women in Entertainment *and* one of its 50 Most Powerful Women in the World.

Me? I eventually had to change agents once more, and my next gig was writing for a claymation show.

Moral? Be nice to junior agents and mailroom employees. They are the future presidents of HBO.

Agents vs. Managers

These days, a lot of people representing talent call themselves managers. The reason for that is, a manager doesn't need a talent agent license and has a lot fewer legal regulations to meet. But they can be just as effective in generating job leads and helping your chart your career.

So, whether you have an inroad to a bona fide agent or a talent manager, do your due diligence and find out everything you can about them. Ask to see their client list and see what kind of credits their clients have. Speak to their current or ex-clients. Ask a lot of questions about how they envision your career. Just be respectful and don't push their buttons. No agent or manager wants to be grilled or answer fifty questions. Be respectful of their time and their interest in you. Make sure you understand their commission structure and what writing of yours is covered. (You don't want to sign of an agent or manager who will only represent you in one slim area – say, sitcom writing – but expects a cut of everything you earn anywhere in showbiz.) If the person has any kind of client list worth noting and the agency/management contract seems reasonable, take the plunge and see where they can take you.

And always remember: 90% of something is better than 100% of nothing.

But, Kevin, *How Do I Find an Agent?* Really...HOW???

Ah yes, I didn't quite answer that one, did I? That's because writers have been asking people like me that question for half a century, and you really think *I* have the magic answer?

Okay, okay – you paid good money for this book, so I'll take a stab at an answer. Here's one way to get an agent, in five (relatively) simple steps:

1. Get a list of 5 LA talent agencies. The Writers Guild publishes a list of franchised (licensed) agencies.

2. Google them. Find the names of their lit agents and those agents' assistants. Then learn as much as you can about **the assistants**. Who is he/she? Where else has she worked? Do you have anyone or anything in common? Facebook them; check them out on Linked In. Stalk them! (Figuratively, of course.) Then whittle your list down to a handful of assistants that sound the most promising.

3. Call said assistants and tell them who you are and that you have a new spec you'd like to get read. They will

invariably tell you that their boss (the agent) doesn't accept unsolicited scripts and then give you some cockamamie story about how to formally submit it through the agency (which means it will never get read). Ignore that advice.

4. Instead, say to the assistant, *"No, you misunderstood me. I don't want your boss to read it. I'd like YOU to read it."* Then explain that you've heard good things about him/her...trying to drop in some tidbit of info you picked up in your research...and say you'd really like the assistant's feedback on your script. Offer to drop it off at the front desk. If they say okay, drop it off **that day**. (Or, if you live out of town, overnight it.) One script in a plain manilla envelop. Attention: (ASSISTANT'S NAME HERE). A simple, *brief* cover letter. That's it.

5. Hope that the assistant's ego and vanity will cause her to be intrigued enough by your call and hungry enough to actually read your script. Here's why...

Assistants move up in an agency by finding talent and bringing it to their boss' attention. If he can spot a hot prospect with a marketable script, that advances his career. Some agencies will even let assistants take on "pocket clients" – an unofficial client that the assistant can try to sell. If he gets you a job or assignment, the agency will sign you officially. So, it's a win-win-win: you get an agency to take a chance on you, the assistant gets a chance to prove he can sell talent, and the agency gets to market your talent at low overhead cost and with no commitment.

This isn't a fail-proof method, but it's the best I've got. My only other advice for landing representation: marry into a CAA agent's family.

ASSIGNMENT

USE MY METHOD TO FIND 3-5 AGENTS YOU THINK WOULD BE RIGHT FOR YOU AND SUBMIT YOUR SCRIPT OR SCRIPTS. (I'D ACTUALLY ONLY SEND ONE AT A TIME. IT'S HARD ENOUGH TO GET ONE SCRIPT READ WITHOUT ASKING FOR MULTIPLE READS FROM THE SAME PERSON.)

BE READY FOR REJECTION. AND KEEP WRITING!

28

HOW A TV STAFF WORKS

Yes, I talked about TV staffs earlier. But that section focused on how TV staffs are hired. What if you luck out and get hired? Here's a look at what you can expect on the job.

Staff writers for the ABC sketch comedy series, "Fridays." Larry Charles (L), Mark Curtiss, Kevin Kelton, Elaine Pope (R)

Every TV series has a writing staff. No, *Curb Your Enthusiasm* was not made up on the set. Larry David always had writing help, even if it was uncredited at first. (In later seasons a few writers' names popped up in the end credits.) Maybe they didn't work like a conventional staff, but no long-running show is ad-libbed or written by one individual. On a streaming limited run series, the show creator may write the first several scripts. But if the run is going to last more than, say, five episodes, invariably he/she will get burned out and the studio will offer to hire fresh hands to carry the load.

Usually, a show has 6-12 writers. The head writer is generally the showrunner(s) – the person(s) who created the series and wrote the pilot. Their title is usually Executive Producer ("EP"). Some shows also have what's called a "non-writing" EP – generally a producer who handles the production side (hiring and supervising the crew, overseeing locations, handling union issues and other non-writing production tasks).

The writing roles and staff titles can include:

- executive producer / showrunner
- more "executive producers"
- supervising producer
- producer
- consulting producer
- co-producer
- executive story editor/story consultant
- story editor
- staff writer (usually uncredited)

Now here's the real pecking order of a TV writing staff:

- the showrunner
- everyone else

That's right. All those fancy titles are just ways to justify paying talented writers more for their years with the show, their value to the show, and to keep them moving up the ladder of success. Say you're a producer on a modest hit series and the show is coming back for its third year. You want a big raise because you've been there two seasons and you've written some very well-received scripts. Your agent may not be able to get you the $10K per show salary bump you request, but he can get you a $5K per show bump and a bump in title to supervising producer. That's how it works. And frankly, those numbers are probably modest.

That's why shows like *The Simpsons* have so many executive producers – after years of being on the air, all the key writers have risen to earn the top credit, even though they aren't the showrunners. Or, if an in-demand writer was an EP on her last show and you want to hire her for yours, you may have to give her an EP credit to close the deal.

Some showrunners may include other producers in casting and editing decisions. Some let other people run the writers' room or take network notes. Like all managers, some EPs are better delegators than others. But make no mistake, the showrunner is the Godfather of the series. Everyone answers to her.

Casting the Writing Staff

The writers' room is an eclectic mix of personalities and talents. Show runners don't just hire individual writers, they try to "cast" the room to make sure they have the array of talents they'll need to get through a long TV season. When hiring for the next season, the showrunner will look to fill holes or perceived weaknesses (similar to how the GM of a sports franchise will draft to fill the needs of his team).

Some writers can be counted on to always turn in a solid first draft. (Not every pro writer can.) Some are better at table work. And some can channel the voices of your characters as if it was themselves.

At *A Different World* we had one Supervising Producer who absolutely channeled Whitley and a few other characters. She could vamp entire half-page speeches off the top of her head while we'd be frantically taking dictation to capture it all.

At *Cheers* they had a very funny guy named Bob Ellison who was a genius at coming up with scene buttons and key jokes when you needed them. At two in the morning, when everyone else was dead tired and dying to go home, Bob could rattle off just the right line for a character with the perfect syntax, timing, and point of view that the scene called for. Because he was so in demand, he could command ridiculous sums of money for just one night a week of room work. And I mean crazy sums – I've heard it quoted at $30,000 a week for one night's work.

Beyond writing talent, the showrunner is also casting the room to see what kind of personalities will gel to create the most creative and cohesive environment. I know writers who are no more talented (and probably less so) than many others, but they keep getting hired because they are amusing, gregarious people that are always entertaining to be around, even at 3:00 in the morning. Showrunners want a staff of people they can see them-selves hanging out with 16-hours a day, five days a week for ten months, because that's exactly what's going to happen. So, it defi-nitely helps to be interesting and pleasant to be around. It's true, some writers get away with being jerks and prima donnas. But only if they are exceptionally talented.

Staff Work: The Daily Grind

Once onboard the show's staff, you'll be working on anywhere from 2-5 scripts at any given time. They are:

1. Polishing and punching up this week's "production" script – the one being shot at the end of this week.
2. Rewriting or polishing next week's script so it's ready for the Monday read-through (for the purposes of this discussion, we'll assume your show works on a M-F schedule).
3. Probably writing your own first draft for an upcoming episode or generating story ideas that can become your next script.
4. Helping other writers work through story problems in their outlines.

5. And, if you're high enough on the writer food chain (a Supervising Producer or higher), hearing freelancer pitches and working with them to get an outline or script out.

So, you'll need to be very good at multitasking and very good at recalling which C-runner is paired with which A-story. Believe me, it can get confusing.

And you'll need to be fast. On a really well-run show you may have the luxury of up to two weeks to write your episode (though that two weeks includes your time spent in the writers' room participating in the nightly staff rewrites – so it's like having two full-time jobs at once). But often, you'll have to turn around a script or full rewrite in a matter of days. I've had to do a top-to-bottom rewrite in two days and generate an original first draft in as little as four.

On those occasions, second guessing and self-doubt is not an option. Neither is a full night's sleep. You just have to do it and trust that what comes out will be good. Most of the time, it is. That's why you got the job in the first place.

I was lucky in that my experience writing for two live series (*Saturday Night Live* and its ABC clone, *Fridays*) prepared me well to deal with the stress of tough deadlines. I don't panic when I get a writing deadline, I just write and get it done. Hopefully you can too.

TV staff hours are long, and it can be very tiring and stressful. But it's more than worth it for the pay, benefits, and perks.

You've probably heard about the legendary free food TV staffs dine on and it's true – the studio has ten people each being paid hundreds of dollars an hour to work, so it doesn't make sense to let them drive off the lot for a 1.5-hour meal when the studio can order in and get them back to work in 20 minutes. So, the studio lets the show gather menus from the best local eateries and order in on rewrite nights – usually two or three nights a week. You've heard of "the freshman 15"? That's nothing compared to the weight gain a staff writer sees after a season of rewrite nights.

Joke patrol: *How to seem off-the-cuff funny...even if you're not*

Yes, TV comedy writing can be financially rewarding and glamorous. But to keep your job you also need to score at the table.

Every writer is expected to carry her/his weight on rewrite nights. Sometimes a script will tank at the Monday read-thru or Tuesday run-thru, and the staff will need to re-break the story (going back to beating it out on a blackboard) and then farming out scenes to be written individually and then collated back into a full draft for a polish pass.

But most nights you're not in crisis mode, you're just punching up the script after hearing it read by the actors or watching a run-thru (a late-afternoon performance after a day of rehearsals).

After watching the run-thru and ordering your dinner, you'll all sit around a beat-up conference table in the writers' room and go page by page, line by line through the script, looking to replace any jokes that didn't work in the read-thru or run-thru. On a good staff, this can be an energetic event with lots of noisy crosstalk and laughter. On a bad staff, this can be a slow and painful experience, as the showrunner goes line by line and implores "Anything? Anything???" while the staff sits in silence.

You don't want to be one of the silent majority. YOU want to be pitching as often as possible. So don't just wait for the meeting and hope ad-lib brilliance strikes. YOU will use your time while everyone else is perusing menus and bickering about where to order from to go through the script and WRITE DOWN as many pitches as possible – including multiple ones for jokes you know died on the floor. Mark up your script. Don't worry if they're not all great jokes – even mildly amusing ideas are better than none when the showrunner or head writer is droning, "Anything? Anyone? *Anything???*" And very often, your half-joke will inspire someone else to build on it, riff on it, until the team turns it into a usable idea or polished line.

The absolute toughest part of the job (at least for me and most writers I know) was when something would die during a taping and the showrunner would turn to the staff for quick pitches to beat it. The live studio audience is waiting, the crew is standing around, the actors are going cold, and your bosses are waiting for you to say something brilliantly funny. Wow, that's pressure!

But if you have the comedy chops and nerve to persevere, it can be done.

Freelance Pitch Meetings

Freelance pitches are very different from staff pitches. If you have a couple of great scripts and can get an agent to rep you, the agent will try to get you freelance pitch meetings. So, let's say you are lucky enough to land an agent and get a pitch meeting. Here's what to do:

1. Freelance pitches are very different from staff pitches. If you have a couple of great scripts and can get an agent to rep you, the agent will try to get you freelance pitch meetings. So, let's say you are lucky enough to land an agent and get a pitch meeting. Here's what to do:

2. Learn the show! It may not be a show you love or have ever even seen. Maybe it's on Nickelodeon and you don't have kids. So, start by seeing as many episodes and reading as many scripts from the show as you can. Your agent may be able to supply a few scripts. But thanks to the web, you should be able to track down a

few more yourself and find several episodes you can watch ASAP.

3. Come up with at least eight (and as many as twenty) story lines. Have at least eight that are full-blown A-stories. Write them out – the logline, inciting incident, act break, block comedy scene, and resolution – and practice delivering them. Make sure there are a few laughs in the pitch. Don't worry about matching A-stories and B-stories - that comes later. But make sure your stories cover most of the main characters (don't only pitch stories that focus on the lead character).

4. At the meeting, make a little small talk when you first sit down and then when they ask what you've got, start with your most unique hook. However, don't start with a pitch that is so out there that it seems like you don't know their series. The first thing you want to convince them of is that you know and understand the show—that you've done your homework. Make sure you know the character names (full names) and the actors who play them.

5. Smile and enjoy the process, even as they are shooting down your ideas, which they will. It's inevitable that they will have already thought of and rejected some of your ideas, or done one in some other form, or they'll kill a few for reasons you had no way of knowing about. (*Joyce's brother comes to visit? That's impossible – Joyce only has one sibling, an identical twin sister and she died in a hot air balloon accident. We established that in the tag of Episode 126.*)

6. Know several beats for each story...a lot more than you plan to pitch. You don't want to pitch everything about the story at first...give the logline and then go back and lay in the details if they like the logline.

7. Anticipate questions that they may ask and be ready with the answer. This is a sort of pitching slight-of-hand and part of the art. If you can anticipate an obvious question that someone will invariably ask – *"Why would Mavis bring a hairdryer to the beach?"* – and be ready with a very good answer, they will be impressed and intrigued.

8. Be ready to vamp. The odds are, if they like a story, they may still want to play with it, move things around, build in other characters, or marry it to another plot line. Don't resist their changes or additions. "Yes, and..." is the key phrase. Everything they say is gold. Laugh at it. Write it down. Love it.

Then hope they buy one idea – either right there in the meeting or with a call a few days later – and be thrilled even if they say they are going to write it in-house and only give you "story by" credit. But hopefully they'll give you a shot at the first draft.

Then you're on your way to outline, then hopefully to script, then hopefully to staff job and a career in television. And this book really begins to pay off!

Failing to the Top

I firmly believe the cream rises to the top. But there are thousands of stories of successful writers (and actors and directors) who failed miserably before they became wunderkind.

Larry David is a great example. When my brother started doing stand-up comedy in the 1970s, Larry was his one of his best friends in the NY comedy clubs, so I got to spend a lot of time around him back then and I know his story well. Larry was a brilliantly inventive stand-up who was just awful on stage. He bombed almost every night. (The comics in the back were laughing, but the audiences just stared...or got hostile.) A few years later, Larry was hired as a cast member and writer on the ABC late-night sketch series *Fridays!*, where I also (coincidentally) wrote for a season. By then Larry had found his comedy voice and was quite funny on the show. But when *Fridays!* was canceled, he decided to give up performing to concentrate on writing full-time, and he had a very painful go of it. He optioned a couple of screen-plays, but nothing got made. He got hired as a writer on *SNL* (where we again worked together, totally by coincidence) but only got one sketch on for the entire season, and he left the show in total frustration. Then he

John DeBellis (L), Larry David and Bobby Kelton (R) at Catch A Rising Star in the 1970s

scrounged around for a few years more until Jerry Seinfeld got a 4-episode sitcom commitment from NBC, and he chose Larry to create the show with him. Up to that point, Larry had only written one sitcom episode, and he was not even close to being a network-approved pilot writer. But with Jerry behind him, he got his "break" fifteen years after starting out in the business.

I know lots of less famous but just as amazing stories of writers who failed and failed until they hit it big. Sometimes you're an also-ran until you're a genius, then sometimes back to also-ran.

Play Nice

Which brings me to my final words of wisdom: be as nice to the little people as you are to the big wigs. I bet you already know why. The guy who was a writers' assistant when I was a producer on *Shaky Ground* went on to be the executive producer of *Family Guy*. The girl who was a secretary on *SNL* became a producer on

Friends and later the showrunner of a series she created. The shy production assistant on *Boy Meets World* became an executive producer on *The Simpsons*. And that mailroomer-turned-junior-agent I told you about earlier, she's still a power-house producer in Hollywood. The people who run errands today will be running shows and networks ten years from now. And they will remember who was naughty and who was nice.

SCRIPT CONTESTS

Students always ask me if they should submit their scripts to competitions. Yes! But only if they are legitimate contests, not money-making scams.

How can you tell the difference? 1) By the entree fee. If it's exorbitant, buyer beware. 2) By who is sponsoring it. If it's a reputable school or company (like UCLA), or a known film festival, great. If it's a screenwriters' website that does nothing but hold script competitions 3-4 times a year, well, all they want is your hard-earned cash/dough/moolah.

Similarly, be leery of script reading services, or worse, people who promise to turn your idea into a full-length script or fix/doctor/polish/punch-up your existing script for a fee. Sometimes they provide a valuable service, but sometimes they are just after your hard-earned cash.

Turning a Job Into a Career

So, say you're lucky enough to write a really great spec. And lucky enough to write another. And lucky enough to procure an agent. And lucky enough to get a freelance assignment or staff job.

So far, you've been pretty damn lucky.

But you can't count on luck – or talent – forever. To turn your first job into a career, you'll need to do five things:

1. **Play nice.** Get along with everyone. Everyone. E-v-e-ry-o-n-e.

2. **Network.** Make friends with your cowriters and, even more importantly, with the studio and network executives (and their assistants). I don't mean, be friendly. I mean, make friends! Lunches are mandatory – try for at least two a week. Socialize with other writers.

3. **Mentor writers.** Offer to read and give notes on their scripts. And when you do, tell them you *love it.* Give honest, helpful notes, but be their biggest fan. Ask your agent to read the best scripts they've come across. And when you find one you really respect, call that writer, and tell him/her. Make friends with great writers. Because great writers become showrunners. And showrunners hire other writers. Often, their friends.

4. **Teach.** You'll be busy, but try to find a program like this one to teach in. You'll be giving back to the writing community. But more important, when you teach, you take the things you know on a subconscious level and define it out loud. And that makes you wiser and better at the craft. As much as you learned in this book, I probably learned as much or more by teaching it.

5. **Get a life.** To write, you need to live. And that doesn't mean going to parties and bars. You'll need a personal life to balance out the work-life. So, stay with your hobbies, or get new ones. Comedy writing may have been your hobby. Now it's your vocation. So, make sure to replace it with something else you love to do in your spare time. Get married and have kids. Because 80% of TV (and half of movies) are about families, kids,

teens, relationships, etc. And those who live it are the best at writing it.

Finally, and most important of all – you guessed it! – keep writing specs!!!!!!!

You can only get so good writing the *Mike and Molly* or *Austin and Ally* scripts you get to write on the staff of those shows. So, unless you landed on *Modern Family* or *Veep* (or a similarly A-list show), use your hiatus to write a new spec or feature.

Lynwood Boomer wrote the spec pilot *Malcolm in the Middle* on a production hiatus 18-years after landing his first job on *Silver Spoons*. He says he wrote it just to keep in practice and to show that he could still write something of quality. That one spec turned his career around.

Even though you've written one or more scripts in conjunction with this book, you probably haven't yet written the spec that will make you a TV giant. You may have it in you. But you'll never know if you don't sit down and write each script as if that's the one. Because one day, it just may be.

Or, as Wayne Gretzky said, "*You miss 100% of the shots you don't take*". So, keep taking shots.

I hope you have a long and successful career, and I see your name in the credits of my favorite show.

I'll be proud to say you were once my student.

FINAL ASSIGNMENT

WRITE – A COUPLE OF SOLID SPEC SCRIPTS FOR EXISTING SHOWS, THEN A SPEC PILOT OR TWO, THEN GET THEM OUT INTO THE MARKETPLACE. BECOME A STAFF WRITER, THEN A SHOWRUNNER, AND MAKE YOUR MARK IN THE TV INDUSTRY.

EXTRA CREDIT – HIRE ME!

RESOURCES

Many of the scripts, beat sheets, outlines, and other resources referenced in this book can be found at https://kevinkelton.com/ links including the *30 Rock* "SeinfeldVision" script, authentic outlines for episodes of *30 Rock* ("Undwindulax") and *How I Met Your Mother*, plus scripts for *Parks and Recreation,* and *Veep*.

But as I advised you in the Author's Note at the the start of this book, ***if you cannot access one of the Assignment an item at that link, substitute it with another beat sheet, outline or TV script you can find online.*** Drew's Script-O-Rama, The Script Lab, DailyScript.com and other sites like them can provide a ton of excellent reading material.

CONFLICT TUNEUP WORKSHEET

A-STORY

My lead character is (focus on *one* character)

_____

His/Her/Their want-need-goal is

_____

As the story begins, s/he is in conflict with

_____

because this person wants/thinks

_____

_____

Two obstacles are
1)_____
2)_____

By mid story, s/he is in conflict with

_____

The story escalates when

_____

_____

The conflict resolves when

_____

_____

B-STORY

This story's lead character(s) is/a

_____

His/Her/Their goal/need/want is

_____

As the story begins, s/he is in conflict with

_____

because this person wants/thinks

_____

Two obstacles are

1)_____

2)_____

By mid story, s/he is in conflict with

_____

The story escalates when

_____

_____

The conflict resolves when

_____

_____

C-STORY

This story's lead character(s) is/are

_____

His/Her/Their goal/need/want is

_____

As the story begins, s/he is in conflict with

_____

because this person wants/thinks

_____

Two obstacles are

1)_____

2)_____

By mid story, s/he is in conflict with

_____

The story escalates when

_____

_____

The conflict resolves when

_____

_____

NOTE: You can fill out a sheet for all subplots.

PARKS AND RECREATION
"SOULMATES" BEAT SHEET
BY RYAN GRASHOW
Reprinted with the writer's permission

ACT ONE
CITY HALL MEETING ROOM
• Chris explains that Pawnee is the fourth most obese town in America and discusses a new health initiative
• Leslie suggest a dodge ball league
• Chris exits the meeting running and Ben adjourns the meeting
• Tom catches Joe from Sewage eyeing Leslie and lets her know
• Joe compliments Leslie and asks her on a date which Leslie passes on

OUTSIDE CITY HALL
• Ron approaches Chris to make sure the new initiative won't interfere with his daily burger ritual
• Chris suggest Ron try a Turkey Burger and explains what a Turkey burger is
• Chris proposes he can make a Turkey burger that tastes better than a hamburger
• Ron accepts this challenge as a cook off - if he wins hamburgers remain in the commissary

OUTSIDE BEN'S OFFICE AT CITY HALL
• Ben tells Leslie he liked the snow globe museum she recommended
• Leslie gives Ben a few ideas she has for the health initiative
• Leslie asks Ben to go to Juju's after work to discuss her ideas and Ben says no awkwardly

LESLIE AND TOM'S OFFICE
  • Leslie tells Ann she asked Ben out and he said no
  • Ann suggests Leslie try Internet dating and offers to help Leslie fill out her profile

RON'S OFFICE
  • Ron asks Ron and April if they want to accompany him to the health food store to get ingredients for his burger
  • Ron states that he's never been to a health food store and accepts Ron's invitation. April offers to join

LESLIE AND TOM'S OFFICE
  • Leslie and Ann review Leslie's results from her online dating profile
  • The site finds a 98% match and Leslie hesitates to look at it while thinking of Ben
  • The match turns out to be Tom

ACT TWO
LESLIE AND TOM'S OFFICE
  • Leslie calls the site's customer service number and tells the rep his service is crap
  • Rep explains about the site's sophisticated technology - he even met his wife there
  • Leslie tells the rep it wont last and that his marriage is a sham

GRAIN N SIMPLE (HEALTH FOOD STORE)
  • Andy asks Chris what various fruits are
  • Chris asks Andy what his favorite food and offers to show Andy a whole new way of eating

RESTAURANT
  • Tom hits on the waitress as she takes their drink orders

• Leslie asks Tom what he likes about the waitress and he explains he likes her boobs

• Leslie confesses to Tom that their profiles matched up on the dating site

• Tom's talking head explains that he has 26 profiles and she matched up with the nerdy one

• Tom's thinks their lunch is a date and is very excited

CONFERENCE ROOM

• Ben goes over health tip ideas with Leslie, Tom, Jerry and Donna

• Tom gushes over the top about his new "relationship" while Leslie tries to share her ideas to Ben

• Leslie takes Tom out in the hallway, yells at him and then kisses him

• Chris sees everything and Leslie pulls the fire alarm to exit the situation, the fire alarm doesn't work

ACT THREE

CHRIS' OFFICE

• Leslie explains to Chris that kissing Tom was a joke

• Chris explains his strict policy against office relationships

CONFERENCE ROOM

• Ben asks Tom what was going on with him and Leslie

• Tom confesses they were matched up on a dating site and he was messing with her but that she's a very good kisser

• Ben cuts him off and tries not to care about the information

COURTYARD

• Chris beautifully presents his turkey burger to the panel in detailing all of the fancy ingredients

• The panel tries his burger and sings its praises

• Ron throws his burgers down on a paper plate and the entire panel changes their tune and immediately embraces the hamburger over the turkey burger

- Ron explains to a flabbergasted Chris that turkey will never beat cow
- Chris explains that he's not had a hamburger in years, takes a bite and anoints Ron the winner

COURTYARD

- Chris approaches Leslie to make sure there are no hard feelings for him making her break up with Tom
- Chris explains how just the other day he had to tell Ben that he couldn't date anyone in government
- Leslie realizes that is why Ben acted so weird when she asked him to dinner
- Leslie approaches Ben and asks if they could go somewhere to talk about her ideas and Ben accepts

PEN15 – outline
"BRACELETS"
By Amanda Maisonave
Reprinted with writer's permission

<u>Cold Open</u>
INT. SCHOOL HALLWAY - MORNING
Maya and Anna walk out of homeroom with report cards.
Anna says her dad will buy her a gift when he takes the girls to
the mall after school if Anna gets straight A's. Anna wants a
Bedazzler, which Maya admonishes until Anna explains that it's
their chance to look hot like Britney, since their moms won't let
them buy BabyPhat. The girls rip open their report cards: straight
A's for Anna and B's for Maya. They dance awkwardly to celebrate. Anna praises Maya, "those B's are bitchin', May!" Maya
chants, "YES Na! You got those straight A's!" Dustin comments,
"Yeah Anna, too bad your chest got all A's too" on his way to
Heather. Maya encourages Anna to ignore him but sees Heather
surrounded by boys, including Alex and Brandt. Anna asks Maya
what Heather has that she doesn't. Maya sees the boys playing
flirtatiously with Heather's jelly bracelets, which appear to glow.

<u>Act One</u>
INT. CAFETERIA - AFTERNOON
Anna asks Maya which stores they should hit up after school,
but Maya is distracted by Heather giving out yellow, orange, and
purple bracelets to her girlfriends. Annoyed, Anna tells Maya to
just ask Heather for one. Maya asks Heather where she got the
bracelets - her older cousin gave her a set because "all the hot girls
are wearing them." Maya asks if she and Anna can have some.
Becca whispers: "Do it! Do it!" to Heather, who claims to only
have blue bracelets left. Anna is uninterested. Heather insists that
Maya take one because "it's Brandt's favorite color." Maya cheeses

when she notices Brandt looking at her and Heather, and she excitedly accepts the bracelet.

At a nearby table, Sam, Jafeer, and Gabe discuss their new comic book, *Weaseldude*. Jafeer notices Maya doing vogue-like poses with her bracelet and looks at Sam: "Dude, why is your girlfriend wearing a sex bracelet?" Annoyed, Sam tells Jafeer to shut up because Maya's not his girlfriend and he doesn't care.

Anna mentions the mall again to Maya, but Brandt interrupts to compliment her bracelet and invite her to get pizza after school. Thrilled, Maya accepts. Anna gives Maya a "seriously?" look to remind her about their plans after school. Maya apologizes and pleads for Anna to be okay with it, promising to hang with her the next day. Anna reluctantly accepts.

EXT. SCHOOL COURTYARD - LATER THAT AFTERNOON

Maya and Anna debate whether or not bedazzling their panties would be hot or just uncomfortable. Anna's dad Curt pulls up, and she proudly shows off her report card. Brandt waves for Maya to join him on the lawn, and she vows to never remove her "lucky bracelet." Anna tells Curt that Maya has other plans and they drive off. Maya awkwardly joins Brandt, Dustin, Alex, and a few other boys. Brandt gives Maya a baby bottle pop. She blushes and tells him it's her favorite candy. Brandt and his friends smirk. Maya removes the plastic and sucks on the candy. Brandt asks Maya how her *head* is. Confused, Maya tells him her head feels fine, but sometimes she gets headaches. Brandt says her bracelet can help because "blue is like, calming and makes your head feel better." Maya doesn't get it. She goes to throw away the plastic in a trash can near where Sam is waiting for his mom.

Sam and Maya greet each other with a "sup." Sam says he noticed
her new bracelet and asks if she's "really into *that?*" Oblivious,
Maya responds, "I mean yeah, it looks really cool and it's
supposed to help with headaches or whatever." Sam tells Maya
he's surprised and doesn't like the bracelet. Maya asks him why
and he says "it just doesn't look right" on her and he thought she
was "different from other girls." Maya, defensive, doesn't get why
he's making a big deal about it. Sam's mom arrives, so he leaves.
Pissed, Maya begins walking back to Brandt. She trips on a stick
and her candy falls on the ground. She picks it up, makes sure no
one's looking, blows on it, and puts it back in her mouth.

INT. ENTERTAINMENT STORE - LATER THAT
AFTERNOON

Curt pulls a copy of *Bedazzled* off the shelf and hands it to
Anna. She laughs and tells him she wanted a Bedazzler. Curt looks
at the cover, revealing a sexy Elizabeth Hurley, and decides to get
it anyway "since we're here." Near the register, Anna overhears
two employees discussing The Sims. She pretends to go get candy
to get closer to them, then picks up a copy of the game. One
employee states, "Dude I made my Sim have the *perfect* life - cool
job, loyal friends, and a bangin' wife, like she's always there for me
and I literally lo...I mean *my Sim* loves her." Anna rejoins Curt and
asks him if she can get the game. Curt goes wide-eyed at the price
and asks Anna if she's sure she doesn't want a Bedazzler instead.
Anna gives Curt puppy dog eyes and tells him Kathy never gets
her cool things like this, but she knows he's the cool parent. Curt
swiftly decides to buy the game for Anna. She jumps around, hugs
him and thanks him.

Act Two

INT. PIZZA PLACE - LATER THAT AFTERNOON

Maya, Brandt, and the other boys split a sausage pizza. Maya
gets sauce on her face. Brandt comments that it looks like she

really enjoys sausage and invites her to his birthday party the next day. Ecstatic, Maya tries to play it cool, then remembers her plans with Anna. She asks if Anna can come so she doesn't have to blow her off again. Brandt responds, "Oh, you sure you don't wanna *blow* her off?" Maya doesn't get it and asks again if Anna can come. Brandt clarifies that they only have room for one more girl to maintain an even number of boys and girls for "activities." Brandt says he can invite someone else if Maya doesn't want to go, but she quickly assures him she'll be there.

INT. MAYA'S LIVING ROOM - EARLY EVENING

Maya arrives home and greets her mom, Yuki, who asks if she picked up Lactaid while out with Anna. Maya explains that she got pizza with Brandt and some other kids after school instead. Yuki remarks that she hopes Maya's change in plans was worth the diarrhea she'll have, and offers to drive her to Anna's the next day for their usual Saturday hangout. Maya says she wants to go to Brandt's birthday party instead. Concerned, Yuki asks Maya if everything is okay between her and Anna. Maya says everything's fine and asks if she can go to the party. Yuki reluctantly agrees to take Maya, and Maya hugs her. While hugging, Yuki sniffs the air, grimaces and comments in Japanese that Maya farted. Maya apologizes and runs towards the bathroom.

INT. ANNA'S LIVING ROOM - EARLY EVENING

Anna creates her first Sim. She sticks out her chest, wishing for bigger boobs, then makes a scantily clad Anna Sim. Anna begins creating a Maya Sim. The phone rings - it's Maya. Anna asks her how her time with Brandt was. Maya says she thinks he's really into her because he invited her to his birthday party the next day. Anna asks if she was invited too, and Maya explains that they were at capacity, apologizing: "Na, I'm sorry, if you don't want me to go, I totally won't, it's just that this is a chance for Brandt and I to take our relationship to the next level." Upset,

Anna tells Maya she should go because she'll be busy playing her new game, since she didn't get a Bedazzler. Both hurt, the girls tell each other passive aggressively to have fun and hang up. Anna deletes her Maya Sim and begins making an Alex Sim. He's a shirtless beefcake.

INT. MAYA'S BEDROOM - LATE MORNING

Maya wakes up and walks over to her mirror to practice flirting with Brandt: "Oh, you like my bracelet? Thanks, yeah, I know it really brings out my eyes" (which are brown). Maya gets closer to the mirror, mouth open and tongue sticking out, imagining she's preparing to kiss Brandt. Yuki knocks on her door and peeks in to check that she's awake because they need to get Brandt a gift before the party. Maya yells that she's up and wants to get him a Blockbuster gift card. Yuki agrees and tells her to hurry up. Maya continues practicing flirting: "Hey baby, I know we just rented this movie but... I don't wanna watch anything but *you*." She starts aggressively making out with the mirror. Shuji, who's been waiting silently at the doorway to troll Maya, comments, "What the fuck are you doing?" Maya yells at him to go away and closes the door in his face as he laughs.

INT. ANNA'S LIVING ROOM - LATE MORNING

After staying up all night, Anna remains glued to the computer. Kathy tries to get her to eat, but Anna irritably refuses because she's "busy actually trying to make her relationship with her husband work." Kathy, confused and offended, asks Anna what she's talking about. Anna ignores her. Kathy gets closer to look at the computer: "What even *is* this game?" Annoyed, Anna tells Kathy, "Nothing. Can you please just go back to taking pictures for your stupid eHarmony profile or whatever?" Kathy can't deal with Anna's attitude and leaves. On screen, the Anna and Alex Sims dance together in their kitchen, which is on fire.

INT. BRANDT'S BASEMENT - AFTERNOON

Maya shyly walks over to Brandt and hands him a card. She
does a voice impersonation of an old woman telling him "not to
spend it all in one place." Brandt gives Maya a "Thanks, cutie"
and winks. She beams, then briefly makes eye contact with Sam
from across the room. She rolls her eyes, then joins the girls.
Heather asks Maya how the bracelet's been. Maya says it's
amazing and her head feels great. Heather points out that Brandt
is staring at Maya. Maya looks up and notices him gesturing for
her to join him in a closet. The girls encourage her to go. Maya
eagerly walks towards Brandt, and Sam looks on in frustration.

INT. ANNA'S LIVING ROOM - AFTERNOON

Anna notices a "play in bed" option on her screen. Intrigued,
she makes sure no one is around, then clicks it. The Anna and
Alex Sims jump into bed and "woo-hoo" under blankets. Anna
smirks, fixated, when Kathy suddenly approaches from behind.
She accidentally startles Anna when she asks her what she's
watching, and Anna freaks from embarrassment, yelling "nothing!" She covers her face and screams at Kathy to get out.

INT. BRANDT'S BASEMENT CLOSET - AFTERNOON

Brandt and Maya stand facing one another, surrounded by
boxes of George Foreman grills. Brandt asks Maya how she wants
to "do it." Maya says she'll follow his lead, ready for him to kiss
her. She closes her eyes, opens her mouth, and begins to lean in.
Brandt moves back instinctively, "Woah...not my face...I think
you missed." Maya asks Brandt what he means, and he points to
his pants. Maya doesn't get it, so Brandt tells her to "just pretend
it's a baby bottle pop." Maya, now understanding, is appalled.
"What the frick? I'm not doing *that*!" Brandt defensively
responds, "What's your problem? I thought you were cool." Maya
retorts that she *is* cool but she's not ready for that. Brandt
reminds her that he's already touched her "nips" and was

expecting her to return the favor, especially on his b-day. Uncomfortable, Maya says he's being gross and walks out.

INT. BRANDT'S BASEMENT - AFTERNOON (CONTINUOUS)

Everyone stares at Maya as she angrily rejoins the group. Brandt follows, "Why are you lying about what you'll do? You're such a tease." Maya, confused, says she isn't. Brandt explains that her bracelet means she'll give a guy a blowjob. Maya, in disbelief, says it's just a bracelet, turning to Heather nervously for confirmation: "Right?" Heather smugly shares that she and her friends only wear colors that mean hugs and kisses because they're not sluts. Maya yells that Heather tricked her into wearing the bracelet. Heather says it's not her fault that Maya lives under a rock. Frustrated, Maya struggles to rip off her bracelet and accidentally backhands Heather in the face, giving her a nosebleed. Maya tries to apologize, but Heather tells her to, "Get away from me, you psycho!" Maya runs up the stairs crying while the other girls tend to Heather. Sam follows Maya.

INT. ANNA'S LIVING ROOM - AFTERNOON

On the computer screen, the Anna and Alex Sims care for their new baby Sim. Anna talks to it aloud: "Me and your dad will *always* be together." Kathy tells Anna to take a break, but Anna yells again to leave her alone. Kathy calls Curt to scold him for buying Anna the game without consulting her. Anna overhears and marches over to yell at Kathy for trying to take away "the one place I can have a happy life!" Kathy tells Anna she's being ridiculous, and Curt continues bickering over the phone. Anna storms off and slams her bedroom door shut. Kathy hangs up on Curt and approaches the computer to see Anna's so-called "happy life." The Anna Sim is naked, eating mac & cheese over the sink.

<u>Act Three</u>

INT. BRANDT'S KITCHEN - AFTERNOON

Sam approaches Maya to console her. Maya asks why he didn't tell her what the bracelet meant. He explains that he thought she knew and was acting "too cool" for him. Maya admits that she's definitely not ready for a BJ when she hasn't even had her first kiss yet. Sam says he's sorry and that Brandt is a douche. Maya asks Sam to leave her alone and she calls Yuki to pick her up, claiming she ate too many cheez doodles and has diarrhea. Maya hangs up and waits in the kitchen alone, where she sees birthday cards from Brandt's family on the fridge. One has a big "14" on the front, revealing that Brandt is a year older than he says he is. Seeing an opportunity, Maya hides the card under her shirt.

INT. ANNA'S BEDROOM - LATER THAT AFTERNOON

Kathy enters with healing crystals and asks Anna what's going on. Anna, still angry, asks Kathy why she can't just let her play The Sims. Kathy asks Anna why she loves the game. Anna says that "everything eventually works out" in The Sims and questions why her parents couldn't just work their relationship out. Kathy pauses for a moment, then asks Anna if the game is realistic.

INT. ANNA'S LIVING ROOM - CONTINUOUS
(QUICK CUT)

The baby Sim, now a toddler in a business suit, is spoon-feeding the Anna and Alex Sims, who are in diapers and bonnets.

INT. ANNA'S BEDROOM - CONTINUOUS

Anna admits that The Sims isn't realistic, but she likes how she can fix things whenever they go wrong. Kathy explains that her relationship with Curt wasn't healthy, and it's not Anna's place to fix it. Anna accepts that relationships are harder in real life. She asks Kathy if she can still play The Sims. Kathy says she can play one hour a day as long as she takes care of herself and remembers it's just a game. Anna agrees and hugs Kathy, who asks when she last showered (she reeks). Anna chuckles and apologizes. Kathy offers to make her Kraft mac & cheese.

INT. MAYA'S BEDROOM - EARLY EVENING
Maya lies in bed crying softly. Yuki enters and asks if Maya wants soup to alleviate her diarrhea. Maya says she just wants to rest. Yuki leaves and Maya picks up the phone to call Anna.

INT. ANNA'S LIVING ROOM to ANNA'S BEDROOM - CONTINUOUS
The phone rings. Kathy answers and Maya asks to speak with Anna. Kathy walks to Anna's bedroom to get her, but Anna is out cold, snoring and drooling. Kathy invites Maya over the next morning without consulting Anna. They hang up. Kathy hears weird noises from the computer and sees Anna's Sims performing a séance.

Act Four
INT. ANNA'S LIVING ROOM - MORNING
Anna and Kathy playfully create a Kathy Sim. The doorbell rings. It's Maya, to Anna's surprise. Kathy leaves to let the girls catch up. Anna is cold. Maya tells Anna she missed her and apologizes for putting a boy before her. Anna remains distant. Maya explains through tears how Brandt called her a tease and liar in front of everyone. This softens Anna: "Oh May, that's *so* effed up. That's like, defamation of character or whatever... We can't just let Brandt get away with it!" Maya admits she knows a secret of his and pulls out the birthday card. Since the girls have been in class with Brandt since Kindergarten, they realize he must have been a repeater. Anna recalls Brandt being strangely good at macaroni art - definitely not a first year's work. Anna suggests writing a threatening note on the card and giving it to Brandt to make him take back what he said. Maya writes "Kindergarten x2, da liar is u! Tell evri I'm no tease, or else! - MIP."

INT. SCHOOL HALLWAY - MORNING

Maya and Anna walk with purpose towards Brant, Maya with the card in hand. A teacher enters the hallway and pulls Brandt aside before class to discuss his failing report card. He's on the verge of tears. Seeing this, Maya softens and decides that sharing his secret right now might be going too far. She shoves the card into her backpack. On her way into class, a few boys intentionally bump into her, calling her a tease, and knock the card onto the floor without her realizing. Sam picks it up.

INT. HISTORY CLASS - CONTINUOUS

Sam slyly passes the card around the class. The teacher obliviously lectures. One kid whispers "Who's 'M.I.P.'?" and another points to Maya while her back is turned. The card eventually gets to Maya, who is confused and mortified. She turns to look at Brandt, who is looking away, teary-eyed.

INT. SCHOOL HALLWAY - LATER THAT MORNING

Maya tries to apologize to Brandt, claiming "no one was supposed to see it." He gives her a dismissive "whatever" and walks away, refusing to speak with her. Heather and the other girls give Maya dirty looks in passing. Maya tells Anna that everything was really Heather's fault, and Anna invites Maya to play The Sims after school to cheer her up. Just down the hall, Heather opens her locker and a mound of blue bracelets with the note "YOU SUCK!" flow out. Anna and Maya laugh and look at each other, confused. Sam looks on from down the hallway and smiles.

Tag

INT. ANNA'S LIVING ROOM - AFTERNOON

On the computer screen, a Heather Sim attempts to leave a room, but a cursor removes the door, trapping her. Maya and Anna Sims eat mac & cheese together, fully clothed, in a bathtub.

Modern Family (aka *My American Family*)

Following are the opening scenes from the pilot script, *My American Family*, by Steven Levitan and Christoper Lloyd, which eventually was renamed *Modern Family*. It is labeled as their Revised 2nd Draft. Only four pages of that draft are re-printed here. The full script can be found at:

http://plexuspictures.com/web/wp-content/uploads/
2015/01/Modern-Family-pilot-script-aka-My-American-Family.pdf

Note that the writers label their opening sequence "First Act." In other series, this might be called the "Cold Open" or "Teaser." But the essential elements, characters and tone of the long-running series *Modern Family* are unmistakeable.

MY AMERICAN FAMILY

"Pilot"

BECAME
"MODERN FAMILY"

Written by

Steven Levitan

and

Christopher Lloyd

Revised Second Draft
December 9, 2008

Characters:

The Dunphy Family

Claire — Late 30s, uptight suburban mom, tries to make everyday special for her kids, needs control.

Phil - Late 30s, real estate agent, upbeat, goofy, thinks he's cooler than he is.

Haley - 16, social, fashion-conscious, rebellious, has a wild streak.

Alex - 13, (girl), smart, cynical, insightful for her age.

Luke - 10, immature, simple, not the brightest bulb.

The Pritchett-Delgado Family

Jay - 60s, successful businessman, divorced. Recently married Gloria, struggles to stay "young" for her.

Gloria - 30s, Hispanic, beautiful, strong, quick-tempered. Protective mother. Divorced six years ago.

Manny - 12ish, Gloria's son - Jay's stepson. Old soul, sensitive, passionate, a young romantic.

Mitchell & Cameron's Family

Mitchell - Mid-to-late 30s, dentist, gay, emotionally restrained, worrier.

Cameron - Mid-30s, gay, free with emotions, lives in the moment, surprisingly strong.

Lily - Baby girl, adopted from Vietnam.

CHANGED TO AN
ATTORNEY
FOR THE SERIES

<u>ACT ONE</u>

FADE IN:

<u>EXT. SUBURBAN AMERICAN STREET -- DAY</u>

The camera pushes in to a SUBURBAN HOUSE.

>   CLAIRE (O.S.)
>   Kids! Breakfast!

<u>INT. KITCHEN -- CONTINUOUS</u>

Claire is busy making breakfast for the family. Phil enters
in workout clothes.

>   CLAIRE
>   What's with the workout clothes?
>   (then)
>   Kids!!!

>   PHIL
>   What? I work out.
>   (glances toward the
>   camera)
>   Just because I don't run six miles a
>   day like you --

>   CLAIRE
>   Eight.

>   PHIL
>   You run eight miles a day? That's
>   like three-thousand miles a year.
>   You could have run to Hawaii.

>   CLAIRE
>   I think about that every single day.
>   (shouting out)
>   BREAKFAST!!!

Haley enters in a short skirt.

>   HALEY
>   I'm having a friend over today.

>   CLAIRE
>   Haley, you're not wearing that skirt.

>   HALEY
>   What's wrong with it?

>   CLAIRE
>   It's too short. People can tell
>   you're a girl, you don't have to
>   prove it to them.

Alex enters.

                    ALEX
               (matter of fact)
          Luke got his head stuck in the
          banister again.

                    PHIL
          I got it. Where's the baby oil?

                    CLAIRE
          It's in our night stan--
               (eyes camera)
          I don't know -- find it!

INTERVIEW -- PHIL & CLAIRE

SUPER: "Phil & Claire"

                    CLAIRE
          Raising kids is like building a car.
          You only have so much time to make
          sure the steering works and the brakes
          stop and the engine is dependable
          before you send it out on the road,
          and if you get one little rivet wrong,
          it will drive off a cliff and explode.

Awkward beat.

                    PHIL
          We have a lot of fun.

EXT SOCCER FIELD -- DAY

Gloria and Jay watch as Gloria's son Manny plays in a soccer
game. Gloria paces around nervously. Jay, dressed in a
track suit, sits in a low folding chair, reading the paper.

                    GLORIA
          Go, Manny, go! Kick it! Don't let
          him -- kick it!

The opposing player trips Manny.

                    GLORIA (CONT'D)
          He tripped him! Where's the penalty?!

                    JAY
          Gloria, they're oh and six. Let's
          take it down a notch.

An opposing player gets the ball. It's only Manny between
him and the goal.

3.

                         GLORIA
                    (while HITTING Jay)
               Get the ball, Manny! Stop him. You
               can do it!

But Manny gets distracted by a PRETTY TEENAGE GIRL riding by
on a bicycle. The opposing player dribbles around Manny and
SCORES. An uptight SOCCER MOM approaches the coach, oblivious
that Gloria is Manny's mom.

                         SOCCER MOM
               Come on, Coach, you gotta take that
               kid out.

Gloria wheels on her.

                         GLORIA
               You want to take him out?! How about
               I take you out?!

Jay grabs the back of her jacket.

                         JAY
               Honey, honey...

                         GLORIA
                    (to Soccer Mom)
               Why don't you worry about your son?
               He spend the first half with his
               hand in his pants.

Gloria moves off, disgusted. Jay, having been through scenes
like this before, shakes his head as A SOCCER DAD approaches.

                         SOCCER DAD
               Whoa, remind me not to mess with
               your daughter.

                         JAY
               My daughter?
                    (annoyed, struggles
                     to get up)
               No, that's funny, actually, no, she's
               my wife. Don't be fooled by the --
               just give me a second here.

INTERVIEW -- JAY AND GLORIA

SUPER: "Jay and Gloria"

                         JAY
               Gloria and I met the day my ex-wife
               moved to Florida. I was feeling pretty
               emotional and Gloria was one of the
               bikini bartenders at the giant pool
               party I threw.

4.

                         GLORIA
              We're very different. Jay is from
              the city, he has a big business, I
              come from a small village, very poor
              but very, very beautiful. It is the
              number one village in all of Colombia
              for the... what's the word?

                         JAY
              Murders.

                         GLORIA
              Yes, the murders.

INT. AIRPLANE - DAY

Boarding passengers file down the aisle passing Mitchell,
who holds on his lap an Asian baby, Lily. As various
passengers pass they smile at the baby and wave.

                         PASSENGER #1
              She's adorable.

                         MITCHELL
              Thanks.

                         PASSENGER #2
              Hi, precious.

                         MITCHELL
                   (waving Lily's hand
                    for her)
              Hi.
                   (then)
              We just adopted her. From Vietnam.
              We're bringing her home for the first
              time.

People across the aisle join in.

                         PASSENGER #3
              She's such a little angel.
                   (to Lily)
              I can just tell you're going to be a
              daddy's girl, aren't you?

Cameron enters and plops next to Mitchell.

                         CAMERON
              Sorry, sorry, this boy needed a
              Cinnabon.

                         MITCHELL
                   (to Passenger #3)
              Let's hope so.

                         END OF ACT ONE

CHARACTER WRITING EXERCISES

Flashback - Write a flashback to an earlier time in your character's life that parallel's what's happening in this story or had an impact on how they will react in this story or how it will unfold. Set it several months or even a year or two before the actual story begins. Put them in a scene with a character that will NOT be in your script. Let them interact in a way that let's you discover some aspects of your character you never knew before. Don't just write it for the sake of writing; try to surprise yourself in the process. Put him or her in a really unusual, highly stressful situation and see how they react. Experiment. Go to weird places — both physically and psychologically. Think of this as the writing version of lifting weights. Put yourself, the writer, under stress by putting your character under stress.

Flash-forward - Write a new resolution to your story that happens 2 days to 2 weeks to 2 years after the end of your script. Make sure something significantly changed in their life or world as a result of your story. If you know where your series character will end up, you will always be writing to a target, be it in season one or season three or season eight.

Phone Call - Write one side of a phone call between your character and someone NOT in the story, either seeking advice on their predicament or trying to solve it. Put roadblocks and obstacles in the call to make it interesting, and to put stress/conflict into the scene.

Love - Write a scene with your character telling a relative stranger they just met about someone they love (or despise). Let him/her open up in ways they normally wouldn't, and say truths only them (and you) will ever know.

Oblique Scene - Write a scene where someone is accomplishing their goal in an unusual way. Example: Father meeting boy who intends to date his daughter. Put them in a setting or situation in which he can intimidate the boy without directly threatening him.

Courtroom - Put your character on the witness stand in their own defense, or have someone testify against/for them. Through cross-examination, let us (and you) learn new things about them, their past, how they react under stress, and how they lie or shade the truth. It's okay if you cross-examine them for a crime they would never commit; the point is to reveal their character through the stress of testifying.

DMV - put your character on a slow-moving line at the Department of Motor Vehicles. See how they deal with the pace (patient, impatient, or gregarious with others on line). How will they deal with the DMV clerks. What interpersonal techniques do they use to get what they want?

Therapy Couch - put your character on a psychologist/psychiatrist couch for a session. Make the therapist some famous real or fictional character. This technique has been used in many series and films, including The Sopranos, Ordinary People, and Good Will Hunting. You could even schedule a weekly therapy session for you and your character to keep you on top of what's happening with her/him psychologically. It's a great ongoing exercise to do parallel with your actual writing of the script. (PS—not everything you learn about her needs to be in your actual script. It's okay – and even desirable – for the writer to know the character better than the audience ever will.)

First Date - Send your character on a first date with another fictional character NOT in their story. Pick a famous fictional character or make one up. And make sure to add stress and conflict to the scene by having their date ask some really pointed, awkward questions. Sometimes a date that's going badly can reveal more than one that goes too well. This is a particularly good way to prepare to write a romantic comedy. If you have seen your character in other dating situations, it will inform you as to how they see relationships and how they react under romantic stress.

Birds and Bees - Have your character explain something very embarrassing they did (or will have to do) to their young children or someone else's children or a kindergarten class. How would they explain the birds and the bees? Or, imagine a ruthless businessman having to explain to his ten-year-old son or daughter how he laid off hundreds of employees and why. How would he justify to a child firing so many people? How would he/she answer the child's innocent yet piercing questions? That could reveal his psychology better than all the board room scenes you could ever write.

ABOUT THE AUTHOR

Kevin Kelton is an Emmy-nominated writer with credits on *Saturday Night Live, Boy Meets World, Night Court,* and *A Different World.* He has also written specials for Jay Leno and Steve Martin, and has penned screenplays and articles for National Lampoon. His novels <u>Super Vows</u>, <u>Pas de Deux</u>, and <u>Things We Shouldn't Do</u> are <u>available on Amazon</u> and other online booksellers.